FARM KIDS

Stories from Our Lives

Billi J. Miller

www.billijmiller.com

Farm Kids: Stories from our Lives

For permission requests, write to the Author at the address below.

E-mail: hello@billijmiller.com

Billi J. Miller
RR #2
Kitscoty, Alberta. T0B 2P0
Canada

Ordering Information:

Quantity sales. Special discounts are available on quantity purchases by corporations, associations, and others. For details, contact the "Author" directly at the address above.

Farm Kids/Miller. —1st ed.

ISBN
978-1-7774186-4-9 (Paperback)
978-1-7774186-5-6 (eBook)

Quotes

"Teaching kids how to feed themselves and how to live in a community responsibly is the center of an education."
– Alice Waters

"I sure want to say hi to those cows, but I don't want to interrupt their yummy silage"
– Kate Miller, 4 years
(While driving with Mom in the car)

"There aren't enough farms in the city."
– Benny Keddy, Nova Scotia, Canada

A Note on the Text & Interviews

The interviews for this book began more than two years before its publication. Therefore, the "age" of the interviewees refers to their age when they answered the questions.

Many interviews occurred during the pandemic, so many were written or held virtually, or in the case of young kids, conducted by their parent(s).

Interviews are edited only slightly to suit print publishing. The text is kept as intact as possible to retain the tone and personality of the subject.

The individuals chosen for this book are random selections of people I've met in real life, virtually, or people referred to me. Interviewees span across Canada and into the United States.

Dedication

For you – who wants to remember.

For you – who never wants to forget.

For you – who wonders what it's like.

And for Gail Verleysen,

April 17, 1991 – September 10, 2021

The truest farm kid there ever was.

Contents

The Author's Story

There's an old oak tree that you can see outside the bedroom window of the farmhouse I never imagined I'd be calling home.

I wanted it that way when we renovated. The tree is slightly crooked but interesting. I chuckle as I think that maybe we have that in common. The story goes that my husbands' grandma Peggy fought with the tree for years to get it to grow. But somehow now – it flourishes.

In case this is the first book of mine you've read; I have fallen deeply in love with farm life. I live on a 111-year-old mixed cattle and grain farm in the Canadian Prairies with my husband and our two daughters.

I came here (to the Earlie District in east-central Alberta) to live in 2010. I had met my husband the summer before while on fishing trip at a lake in Northern Saskatchewan. We were both 34 when we met.

I like to think I enchanted him with my fishing skills, then I let my sense of humour do the rest. Teach a man to fish, they say... okay, that's not entirely true, but we did fall for each other quite quickly.

I had been living in the city for sixteen years before my move to the farm eight months after meeting him, so you could say farm living was certainly not in my prior plans.

Since about a month into our relationship, however, he and our relationship became the plan.

Dean Miller was a farmer. But not just any farmer. He's a born-in-a-plaid-shirt, sure of-his-life's-path, never-questioned-where-he'd-spend-his-life kind of farmer.

We married in October of 2010, and since that time, I've settled into life on the farm and have made it my own. The beauty of being 34 when you meet your significant other is you already have a strong familiarity of yourself to know what you would like in your life to be happy.

I've carved my own role here to be a "mostly" comfortable mixture of caring for our two girls, our life, and running the business I started in 2012 as a freelance and contract writer and photographer. Since becoming an author, I've added the role of event speaker, too. On top of that... there's farm life.

Most days, I revel in the fact that I have a family I adore and a career I've always dreamed of.

Our farm now was the family's original homestead. Dean is a fourth- generation farmer, and this land was settled by his great-grandad in 1911.

This yard where we and our kids now live is well-established by spruce trees planted by my father-in-law and his sisters following their mother while she led. Another row of spruce trees was planted by Dean and our neighbour Charlie (who, coincidentally, is responsible for introducing us).

Our home is a complete renovation of his grandparents' 1965 new build. In this house, Dean and I have built our own vision and dreams.

Behind our house is a huge grove of maple trees where our kids play amongst the treasures left behind by generations before them: bottles, old rusty cans, and whatever else was deemed fit in their imaginations.

I've become so attached to this place. Not just our yard, but the "neighbourhood" too. I've become close to many in this community over the years.

As of now (summer of 2022), I've lived here twelve years. This is longer than I have lived anywhere – ever.

I really have never had a "home" to go back to from my childhood. My family of origin changed on a number of occasions (due to several parental divorces), and so "home" and "family" has been something I have had to create for myself.

Living in this place has filled holes in me that I never knew existed. Getting used to people being there for me, our family, and my children has been balm for my soul. And, allowing it to become the "home" I've always wanted has healed me in ways I never knew I needed.

The Farmwives Books

I used to dream of writing books. Well, that profession alongside a traveling photographer with National Geographic.

When I was a kid, I would write books that I'm sure were more of a re-write of the "Sweet Valley High" novel I was reading at the time than a work of original art. However, I wrote them nonetheless, and stapled them together to bind them.

When my married life settled me into the country, rather than the city, I knew that what I chose for employment would require creativity.

Although much of my work supports our farm business, after having my first daughter, Madeline, I knew that my work as a writer and photographer is what had my heart. I began taking photographs primarily of farm families and wrote stories for the local newspapers.

Fast forward ten years, that experience has led me to publish three books, and you're now reading the fourth.

My first two books, referred to as "The Farmwives Books" (www.billijmiller.com/farmwivesbookproject) hold a special place in my heart. The first: "Farmwives in Profile: 17 Women, 17 Candid Questions About their Lives, Photos & Recipes" feature women from my community and just outside of it. They are all between the ages of 55 and 90 and fulfill the role of "traditional farmwife."

My purpose of that first book was to shine a light on farm women for their remarkable contributions to not only their homes, families, and farms, but also to Canada's cultural heritage. These women in my community touched me so much upon moving here. Although humble, they are the pillars holding up their communities. What a legacy that is.

My second book, "Farmwives 2: An Inspiring Look at the Lives of the New Canadian Farmwives," was a continuation of that story – only this time, I wanted to home in on the stories of younger women than in the first book. So, these women hailed from across Canada, and their stories focus on the innovative and sometimes, non-traditional ways women are carving their path on their farms.

Ultimately, my first two books celebrate the richness, diversity, and pivotal roles filled by women no matter what work they do. I do believe they are the hearts of the farm and of this whole industry.

That brings me to why I'm here now writing my fourth book for you.

Why tell the story of Farm Kids?

"Being raised a farm kid is the best gift ever received." - Unknown

I have never met a single person that was raised on a farm that didn't speak highly of the experience. Not one.

Whether that is a "kid" of the present, a boy, or a girl, or whether that "farm kid" is now a 90-year-old man reminiscing on his childhood in the 1930s. Their memories are strong, often comical, and the fondness is real.

I came up with the idea for this book well before the pandemic. Writing it during the pandemic, however, has been a struggle. Not only because I've been a "working parent" in the trenches like many of you, but also because I've been simultaneously witnessing the divide that many of our communities have experienced throughout this past two-and-a-half-years. If I'm being honest, I've had moments where it's worried me for how we'd all go on.

But if there's one thing the pandemic has done for me – and hopefully most of us – it's reminded me to look outside of myself and has put what's important into perspective.

I feel so incredibly lucky to live where I live. This farm became the home of David Miller in 1911 when he came from Scotland to claim this homestead as was done in that day.

This is a green quarter set beside a ravine with rolling hills and many stories. I'm grateful that our daughters are being raised here hearing those stories and making many of their own.

In my heart of hearts, my reason for writing this book is threefold.

One, for my daughters. I want to somehow capture for them some of the nostalgia from their childhood. I hope they read this book decades from now and fondly remember their life on the farm.

Next, for farmers. I want to remind all of us why we do what we do and live how we live. Even through challenging times, I hope this book brings us all hope and remembrance of why we live this life. I hope it gives us hope that we can mend the tears that may have occurred in our communities these last two years.

Third, for non-farmers. I hope this book helps to dispel some myths you may have thought of the farming community. The last chapter shares some of the thoughts communicated by hundreds of farmers when I asked them: "What do you wish non-farmers knew about us?"

Thank you for reading this book.

Kate Miller, Alberta

Year born: 2013

"Kid from Today"

Photo by: Billi J. Miller

What kind of farm do you live on?

Beef and crops.

What is the best part of living on a farm?

That I have a big yard.

Tell me the best thing about your Mom.

She gives me hugs whenever I need them.

What is the coolest thing about your Dad?

That he shows me how to drive tractors.

Have any pets?

Bubbles, Cheese, Wink, Shadow, and an orange fluffy cat that randomly showed up.

What's the coolest machine on your farm?

Our combine. It's a CLAAS.

What do you want to be when you grow up?

A farmer, a teacher, or a vet, or all three.

One last thing, what do you think it would be like to live in the city?

Horrible except I could order anything on Skip the Dishes, and it could come to my door.

Bob Stone, Alberta

YEAR BORN: 1930

"KID FROM THE 30S AND 40S"

Bob Stone (October 9, 1930 – September 19, 2020). Photo by: Billi J. Miller

Where did you grow up? How many siblings do you have?

I was born in Islay, Alberta, but I lived on our farm all my life until we moved to nearby Lloydminster in May 2013. I have one sibling, a sister named Betty who was five years younger than I.

What kind of farm did you grow up on?

A mixed farm. We had cattle, pigs, chickens, and ducks at one time. Also, we grew wheat, barley, and canola. This was my Grandpa's homestead. My grandparents lived on the farm, too.

What are your key memories of your Mom?

She was always there looking after us. She was a good cook. She belonged to groups like the Ladies' Aid and the Red Cross. She used to get together with Aunt Blanche and the Ladies' Aid ladies to tie quilts. They sent parcels to the soldiers during World War II of knitted socks.

Tell me about your Dad.

Dad was good too. He was on the Municipal Council for 23 years. When he started out, there were no roads in the county, just trails. So, he built lots of roads in the County of Vermilion River #24.

What was a typical day for you after you got home from school?

I helped with farm work. I drove the tractor (John Deere) on the binder in the fall. My father rode binder. I remember one wreck – I got to the top of the hill (not quite) and couldn't hold the brake down because I

wasn't heavy enough. The tractor rolled back and jack-knifed into the binder. It broke the slat on the reel and poked a hole in the tire. So, we went home, fixed it, and went back to work.
I did chores – fed the pigs and threw hay to the cattle and horses.

What do you remember doing most on weekends?

I pretty much always had a ball game on the weekends. In Wildwood, Earlie, Kitscoty or Paradise Valley. We chased girls. We went to church. People came to skate in the wintertime. We built bonfires.

What's the biggest way you think farming has changed in your lifetime?

That's a big question. It's changing every day. We had a two-cylinder John Deere tractor when I was young and a much bigger one in the end.

We thrashed until 1952 and had to stook the grain. We got a Massey 26 combine from June's parents in 1955 or 1956.

We could plow 10 acres daily with a two-bottom plow on a tractor.

What did you like best about farming when you were younger?

Harvest time because that's when you found out if you made any money.

What other memories do you have that stand out?

In 1950, I took a six-week welding course in Edmonton. From 1936 to 1944, I attended Wildwood School in my area. I walked about one and a half miles to school. When I was nine or ten, I was wrestling with Ray Wheadon and fell down, got my arm stuck down a gopher hole, and broke my arm. I was taken to Islay Hospital, where a cast was put on. I stayed there for a couple of days.

There were lots of gophers in the school, and as kids, we spent recess and noon hours drowning and snaring them. We'd pour water down one hole, and the gopher would come up another one.

We would play Anti-I-Over at the school. We played ball on the hillside. We batted up the hill, so we didn't have to chase many long balls or hits. No home runs here.

We carried our lunches to school in a Rogers Syrup pail. Our lunches were usually bread and meat, or jam sandwiches, sometimes a cookie or cake and an apple or orange.

Claire Nagel, Saskatchewan

Year Born: 2006

"Kid From Today"

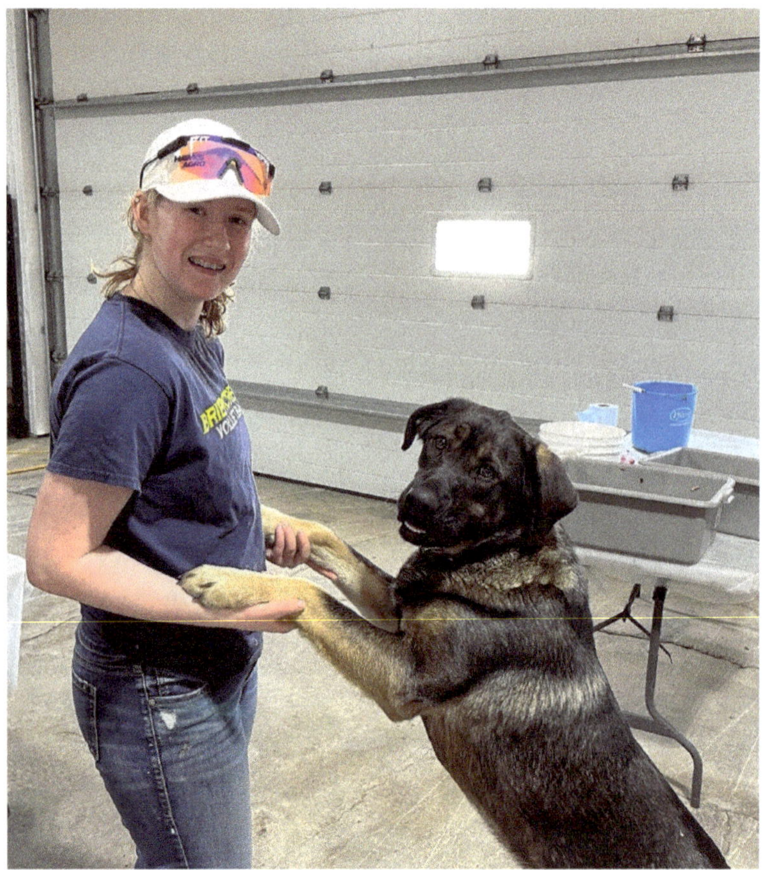

Photo supplied.

Where do you live? How many siblings do you have?

I live on a farm outside the small town of Mossbank, Saskatchewan with my Mom, Dad, and younger sister Addison. My sister and I have grown up playing sports, joining many clubs, and helping on the farm whenever possible.

What kind of farm are you growing up on?

I am growing up on a farm that produces crops such as durum, canola, lentils, and barley.

Tell me about your Mom.

My mother, Cherilyn Jolly-Nagel, was born and raised on a farm five minutes outside Mossbank. Growing up, she swore she would not be a farmer.

My mother is now a farmer, but not only that. My Mom travels all over North America, educating the public about modern agriculture, food production and security.

My mother is a member of the Sask Power Board of directors, one of the 50 most influential people in Canadian agriculture, and an amazing volleyball cheerleader!

Tell me about your Dad.

My father, David Nagel, owns and operates Hunters Paradise farm. Unlike my Mom, he always knew he would be a farmer; in fact, he had already bought a house on the farm before he graduated high school.

My Dad is an amazing cook; he can whip up anything! He is also an amazing teacher. He taught me how to drive the grain cart, the land roller, and the combine.

Describe a typical day after you get home from school. What do you do on a typical weekend?

When I get home from school, I do all the work that has to be done inside first to avoid all the more taxing physical labour. Then, when there is no other way to procrastinate, I go outside and feed the rabbits, the cats, the dogs, and the horses. After this is done, it is off to whatever sport I have that day.

On weekends and during summer vacation, I run the land roller for my Dad during seeding, and I run the grain cart during harvest.

What kind of jobs do you have on your farm? How do you think your life differs from your friends who live in town?

As I mentioned, my jobs on the farm include feeding animals, making supper for the crew in the field, and primarily, being in the field. Running the grain cart during harvest is my favourite job by far! Living on a farm has given me a good work ethic and a very good perspective on what it is to work hard. I am so grateful to have been raised on a farm, and to have been given the opportunity to learn through example what it is like to own and operate a business.

What is the thing you love most about living on a farm?

The thing I love most about growing up on a farm is the opportunities that have been available to me. I've had many jobs on the farm, as well as working at the local John Deere dealership, and waitressing at the only restaurant in our small town.

How do you feel being raised on a farm helps to shape you and your future?

Being raised on the farm has given me a fantastic work ethic and a great attitude toward physical labour. Who I am and what I will become is a product of how and where I was raised. I have my parents to thank for everything I have done and will ever do.

If there was one key thing you wish non-farmers would know about farmers or farming - what do you wish it was?

One thing I wish "city folk" would understand about living on the farm is how open and amazing it is! The sunsets cannot be compared to the lights in the city! One other thing people should know is that we really don't just hold pitchforks.

Karen Fawcett, Alberta

YEAR BORN: 1972

"KID FROM THE 80s"

Photo supplied.

Where did you grow up? How many siblings do you have?

I grew up in Consort, Alberta, with four siblings. Three brothers, Bruce, Todd, and Ryan, and one sister, Lana.

What kind of farm did you grow up on?

I grew up on a mixed farm, where we grew grain and raised cattle. There were chickens, pigs, and wild boars through the years, but the cattle remained a constant.

(Fun fact: I have never been chased by a cow. I have been chased by a chicken, so I'm happy to see them on the table on any given day. Mean little buggers!!)

What key memories and qualities come to mind when you think of your Mom?

My Mom. My Mom is an angel. I am sure of it. My Mom knows exactly what to say and do when you need advice. She handles any situation thrown at her with dignity and grace. She never flinches, even when you tell her your deepest secrets.

She is the epitome of unconditional love. Somehow, even though she is not a priest, nor are we Catholic, she is able to grant absolution because once you unburden yourself to Mom, (or Mumsey as we affectionately call her), the hurting, the anxiety and the fear all stop. All is forgiven and forgotten, and you know everything is going to work out fine...all because you have talked to Mumsey. Her hugs heal you.

Mumsey is practical and wise. She is our family's caterer, chauffeur, laundress, moneylender, seamstress, psychologist, tutor, nurse, etc. She is dedicated to our family, her husband, our farm and even found it in her heart to have a soft spot for our family dog, Lily... who was brought home even after Mumsey had made it very clear that she was not having another dog in the house. It only took her three days to speak to my Dad and I again. We patched that up.

Mumsey is devoted to her family. She is kind, honest and has a huge heart. Her heart understands what you cannot say. Mumsey is a strong woman and works tirelessly for any cause she believes in. She is a shoulder to cry on and a pillar of strength for all of us. She is the glue that holds us all together.

Mom told me that after she became a mother, she felt like she had found her niche in life. I believe she did. She is the best mother and friend anyone could ask for, and I am so grateful that God gave her to me.

Tell me about your Dad.

My Dad is my hero.

It is that simple. He is a man that I am very proud to call my father.

As a little girl, I always wanted to go with my Dad -- in the tractor, in the truck, in the shop, off to town, off to choir practice. Dad was always doing something that was new to me, and because I spent a lot of time with him, I learned many skills on the farm.

My Dad is honest, fair, and kind. He loves his family and is always rooting for the underdog. He is a steadfast friend to many, and I have witnessed this strength of character many times. He stood beside his friends and family when the going got tough and saw them through, when many simply turned their backs on the situation.

Dad loves farming in every sense of the word. He knew he wanted to farm at a young age and is the third generation of farmers on our land. He has a keen interest in history and delights in watching the old tractors, threshing machines and cats being used in demonstrations and sometimes even used on the land. I gave my Dad a plaque one day, when I was about eight years old. I found it at the Meier Variety Store in Consort, and the poem on it was entitled, "Thanks Dad." It was a poem written by Frank Pavlick and Dad has it hanging on the wall beside his desk. To read the whole thing makes me cry, but the last line always sticks in my mind, and I think of it often. It reads, "Although I may not know too much, one thing I clearly see, When God made out his list of Dads, The Best, he gave to me."

What was a typical day like for you after you got home from school? What do you remember doing most on the weekends?

What was a typical day like when I got home from school? Well, that depended on what day it was! For years, Mondays, we drove 90 miles to Stettler for singing lessons and choir, Tuesdays, we had piano lessons, Wednesdays, we had Junior and Senior Choir and I do believe Thursdays were free...unless I'm forgetting something.

However, after arriving home, we would sit down with Mom and have a visit, and then help with supper preparations or set the table. We would have supper, and Dad would come in and ask us about our day. He would ask us what we learned today, and as typical kids, our response was always, "Nothing." After supper, there was always TV to be watched or homework to do.

I was supposed to practice piano, but I feel like I could count on one hand how many times that happened. My poor parents. Talk about throwing good money after bad!

If we were home right after school, we would rush into the house, turn on Channel 10 CKRD and watch Samantha Taylor and Video Hits! That was a big deal! Some nights in the wintertime, I would go out to fork up hay to the calves, and many nights, I would go out to the corrals and hold the gates for my brother while he put straw bales out for bedding. It was at this time that I would at least practice my singing. The calves made an excellent audience, and my brother couldn't hear me singing over the noise of the tractor. That worked out well for me!

On weekends, I would look forward to it raining in the spring, because that usually meant that Dad was free, and we could go to Red Deer and go shopping! That was my favourite! It meant a stop at the M-m-m-muffin stand and Orange Julius! Dad always made sure we brought a box of muffins home too!

Some weekends meant we would be branding calves, cultivating, rock picking or those sorts of jobs. Keeping the lawn cut became my job when I was about 12, and I still hold the title of "Yard Marshall" at home. Weekends also meant housecleaning, cleaning our rooms and vacuuming. I would try to escape outdoors as much as I could. When I was about twelve, I would take my dad's truck and drive it around and around the farm, practicing driving and seeing if I could get going fast enough to need third gear! That was a good time! I had a good track that went around the corrals, through the yard and out by the bins. AM106 was the best radio station, and my sister and I spent many hours listening to it, calling in to vote for the competitions and driving our mother crazy, while she had to listen to "those drums that they are beating to death" in every song.

Weekends were mostly spent at home on the farm, amusing ourselves and finding stuff to do, or helping out with chores. I had three older brothers, so the farm work was mostly looked after by them and my Dad.

Mom helped on the farm too, and when she was out, I was "Chief Cook and Bottlewasher." I remember making my first dinner for everybody when I was ten that consisted of ground beef, green pepper, rice, pineapple, and onion. I felt so grown up. It was the first time I had made a meal, and we didn't even have to bury it in the backyard!

What would you say was a key activity you did to entertain yourself as a child? As a teen?

A key activity that would have entertained me as a child would probably have been playing with my sister, Lana. We liked to slide around on the linoleum floor in our socks, slide down our carpeted stairs in polyester pants for a fast ride... which later resulted in bruised tailbones. We went out and played in the bales, jumping from bale to bale, and roughing up the tops of them. We picked potato bugs for money, not necessarily entertainment! We would air band and make up dances to Abba, Air Supply and Tanya Tucker, which involved complicated gymnastic moves and the rocking chairs in the living room. I loved playing with my baby dolls, and my sister loved playing with her Barbies and reading.

As teens, we would listen to the radio, tape songs off the radio, drive around the farm, sing and play a little piano. We would sometimes go to hockey games to mostly chase boys, and that worked out about as well then as it has now! I would spend hours in my room listening to whatever rock music or musician I had become obsessed with, and there were many: A-ha, Led Zeppelin, Robert Plant, John Mellencamp, Bruce Springsteen, Neil Diamond, and Tom Jones to name a few! Trying out different makeup styles was a fun pastime. Talking on the phone with friends also took many hours out of the day. Daydreaming was something I was particularly good at.

What did you like best about farming when you were younger?

I liked the fresh air all the time, the freedom to go and drive wherever you wanted around the farm. I loved the fact that we always had bottle baby calves in the spring, and we could play with them whenever we wanted to, and they would always come running to us. Little did I know at the time, it was because I had their food, I just thought they were genuinely happy to see me!

I liked being able to run the machinery, and I liked helping with moving equipment from field to field when needed.

I liked being able to drive to town for parts -- my record was six times in one day! I liked going out and being able to be with my family, and I was never lonely as I had my parents, siblings, and pets around to keep me company.

Did you feel brothers were treated differently than sisters in your family? Were expectations different?

My brothers were older than I was, and therefore they had more responsibility than I did regarding outside work and chores. I remember the first time I helped brand calves; I was ten years old. We were heeling them at that time. My brother Todd held the back leg, and I was to hold the front leg and keep my knee on their neck to keep their head down. I had no idea what I was in for. I guess I got to help because I was old enough and strong enough to be more of a help than a hindrance. I watched with eyes like big saucers as my Dad castrated the calf. I had no idea what was even going on.

I remember my Dad saying to my brothers, "Watch your language...we have a lady out here." The other thing I remember was my Dad taking one look at my face and saying, "Oh Dude, I guess you haven't seen this before, have you?" I shook my head wild -- not knowing if I ever wanted to see it again either!

Meanwhile, my sister Lana was sitting on top of the corral fence, watching from a safe distance. Mom and Dad asked her to get down off the fence and come and help. She was eight.

She said, "NO. I may not have been born a city girl, but I'm sure going to live like one." From that day on, I always knew Lana was smarter than me. LOL!

I am lucky to be from the farm that I am. We didn't have jobs reserved "just for the boys" and "just for the girls." If you could do the work, operate the machine and/or were willing to try, you could do whatever had to be done. This is how I learned to bale, swath, run a cultivator, disc, weld, drive trucks, pack the silage pit, work cattle, harrow, you name it. That's how it was learned, and that is something I'm very proud of.

How do you feel being raised on a farm helped shape you and your future?

Being raised on a farm helped to shape me in many ways. It gave me a strong work ethic and a practical view of the world.

I'm proud of how I was raised and being from small-town Alberta, and to have been a farm kid. I still love the farm. I go back every chance I get and help out with whatever needs to be done. My experience on the farm has given me much fodder for my Darling Diva musical performances, and I love the fact that most of my audiences can relate to my experiences too.

Being a farm kid has made it easy to tell the difference between shit and shinola(or sort the wheat from the chaff if you need a better expression!)

If there was one key thing you wish non-farmers would know about farmers or farming, what would it be?

I wish that non-farmers understood that "dinner" is served at noon and "supper" is served at night!!! That drives me nuts!!!

Farming is a mindset, a labour of love, and a way of life. It never leaves you, and I am eternally grateful to my parents, my grandparents, and my great-grandparents for settling our family where they did and providing us with the best life possible.

I have a ring I wear, with our home quarter land location engraved. That land location is where home is, our farm and my heart will remain.

No truer words have been spoken than, "You can take the girl out of the farm, but you can't take the farm out of the girl."

Gary Miller, Alberta

Year born: 1949

Kid from the 60s

Photo by: Billi J. Miller

Where did you grow up? How many siblings do you have?

I was born to David "Dudley" and Peggy Miller in 1949 and was raised on our farm twenty minutes southwest of Lloydminster, Alberta/Saskatchewan. I have three sisters: Della, Madeline (Duffy) and Sharon.

What kind of farm did you grow up on?

Mixed, cattle and grain. We had pigs and ate like pigs too. My mom had chickens, a peacock, guinea hens and donkeys. My dad had a mule team.

What are your key memories of your Mom?

Saturday mornings, the radio playing and Mom and my sister Sharon baking in the kitchen humming.

Tell me about your Dad.

My dad was like any other dad. Your kids feel like they know so much more than you. He was an easy-going guy; he didn't worry about money. They liked to go to dances two or three times a week. They played a lot of cards.

What was a typical day like for you after you got home from school?

Start chores, had a snack of toast. I hauled water to the pigs, got the cows in and cleaned the barn.

I biked to "Earlie School" from grades one through six. Then, from grades seven through nine, I went to the school in nearby Paradise Valley, Alberta.

I had an old Democrat I used to ride down a hill on while I was sitting on the axle.

What do you remember doing most on weekends?

I would clean out the pig barn and do chores. I would get ready to go to town. I would visit the drug store or Matheson's Groceteria with Ellen Rompage. We would go to movies in Paradise Valley.

What is the biggest way you think farming has changed in your lifetime?

I think it would be the change in tractors. It's gone from sitting in the dust and getting sunburnt to sitting in an air-conditioned cab.

What did you like best about farming when you were younger?

Everything. The freedom.
We used to sleep up in the hay loft all summer. We used to try to ride the pigs.

What do you think we as farmers are doing well now?

Spending money -- ha-ha!
Learning how to market your own grain when we just hauled it to the Wheat Board.

What kind of things do you wish we were doing more of?

Oh, I don't know! It's funny at our age as a dad, you look at what your kids are doing, and if it's not how you did it – you think they're doing it wrong.

Kaitlyn Kitzan, Saskatchewan

Year born: 1998

"Kid from the 2000s"

Photo submitted.

Where did you grow up? How many siblings do you have?

Theodore, Saskatchewan. I have one older brother, and we are three years apart.

What kind of farm did you grow up on? What was your job on the farm? Do you still work there?

I grew up on my family's cow/calf and grain operation. Growing up, my job was to check cows and help with yard work. Since I moved away for university, I have always come home to help when I can, especially during calving and harvest time. Our family is currently going through succession planning, and my brother and I will be a part of the farm corporation.

Tell me about your Mom.

We call my Mom the CEO of the farm, The Chief Emotional Officer. My Mom has worked full-time off the farm as a nurse in Yorkton, SK, and is currently in her 41st year of nursing! Even though she worked full time off the farm, she also worked full time on the farm, providing meals, doing housework and yard work and being a taxi driver for my brother and me.

Tell me about your Dad.

My Dad looks like a big mean bear, but he is truly a teddy bear. He is a workaholic; however, he would never miss any activities of mine and my brothers growing up. You can find him in the evening reading the latest Western Producer staying on top of the latest agriculture news or scrolling Kijiji ads to buy or sell machinery. He is very passionate about farming and has dedicated his whole life to the family farm.

Describe how a typical day looked after you got home from school? What did you do on a typical weekend?

Most days, I didn't get home from school until 9 p.m. because I was involved in many extracurricular activities. It seemed like I was always running from a music lesson to dance classes to 4H club meetings or basketball practice. On the weekends, it was my time to catch up with school and hang out on the farm. However, in the winter, I was a Hockey Sister and spent most weekends on a hockey bus travelling across Saskatchewan and cheering on my brothers' team.

How do you think your life differed from your friends who lived in town?

If I wanted to hang out with friends, it had to be planned in advance because we were expected to catch the bus after school every day if we didn't have extracurricular activities. I also think I had more responsibilities as a kid, such as farm chores, than most of my friends in town.

What is the thing you loved most about living on a farm?

The animals. I have been an animal lover since I was a kid, owning my first horse at three years old. I would have had every type of animal on the farm if my Dad had let me. Looking back, I loved the freedom of farm life. The farm was and still is my happy place. It was the place where I could truly be myself.

How do you feel being raised on a farm helped shape you and your future?

Being raised on a farm has helped shape me into who I am today. It taught me the importance of hard work, responsibility, determination, and many other essential leadership skills early in my life. My passion for the farm has also led me to a rewarding career in agriculture.

If there was one key thing you wish non-farmers knew about farmers or farming, what would it be?

I wish people of all ages took the time to learn and gain awareness about how their food is produced right here in Western Canada. We take so much pride and passion in growing food for the world. Trust us.

Sam Purser, Alberta

Year born: 2012

"Kid from Today"

Photo supplied.

What kind of farm do you live on?

Cattle and grain.

What is the best part of living on a farm?

That you get to check cows a lot. Always new calves.

Tell me the best thing about your Mom.

Her caramel and grilled cheese.

What's the coolest thing about your dad?

He coaches me at stuff.

What's the coolest machine on your farm?

The seeder. Me and my dad and Grampa work on all the hoses.

What do you want to be when you grow up?

Me and Carys (sister) want to be farmers. She has a heifer, then I'm going to get a blonde heifer, then we're going to get two bulls. We're going to keep one of ours named Jack (he's brown), and we're going to buy a white bull.

Conversation between Mom, Sam, and Carys sometime in 2015:

Mom: Sam, what do you want to do when you grow up?

Sam: Farmer

Me: What about you Carys?

Carys: Um, let me think.
(Long Pause)

Sam: A cow?

Ceriel Mauws, Alberta

Year born: 1925

"Kid from the 30s"

Photo by: Billi J. Miller

Where did you grow up? How many siblings do you have?

I grew up on the NE-16-48-3-W4 (in the Earlie District of east-central Alberta), the same quarter my Dad homesteaded in 1910. I had a half-sister, Margaret.

What kind of farm did you grow up on?

It was a mixed farm. We grew wheat, oats, and barley. We also had a cow-calf operation. We kept our steers and fed them out, selling them as three-year-olds. We used some of the heifers as replacements and sold the rest of the yearlings.

What are your key memories of your Mom?

I remember my Mom as kind and gentle. She always grew a good garden and had a green thumb. She was known as Nanna to her grandchildren and the children in the surrounding districts.

Tell me about your Dad.

Dad came from Belgium at the age of twenty-two, taking care of cattle on a cattle boat in exchange for free passage. He worked for a Belgian family before coming to Canada and homesteading the NE-16-48-3-W4 in 1910. Dad sold seed oats for many years and became known as the "oat king." He shipped oats as far east as Manitoba. Dad farmed this land until his passing in 1959.

What was a typical day for you after you got home from school?

My first three years of schooling were in Earlie (my district), then I attended Clandonald Convent School from 1935 to 1940. When I came home from school, I had chores like bringing in firewood and water and checking on my pet kittens.

What do you remember doing most on weekends?

I remember weekends of playing ball, riding horseback, and snaring gophers.

What is the biggest way you think farming has changed in your lifetime?

I have seen farming change immensely — from horses to tractors, electrification, hydraulics, equipment size and technology. Major recent changes are the switch to no-till, the improvements in chemicals and other inputs, guidance systems and grain handling systems.

What did you like best about farming when you were younger?

I have always enjoyed harvest time. It is a payoff for a lot of hard work.

What do you think we, as farmers, are doing well now?

I think farmers now manage their farms, protect the land, and look after their livestock well. I also think they are raising their families in a good environment close to nature.

Carson Green, Saskatchewan

Year born: 2008

"Kid from Today"

Photo supplied.

Where did you grow up? How many siblings do you have?

I'm the fifth generation on my family's farm west of Mossbank, Saskatchewan. I have three siblings: one sister and two brothers.

What kind of farm are you growing up on?

A grain and cattle farm. We grow crops such as canola, durum, chickpeas, and lentils. On the cattle side of the operation, we raise black Simmental/Angus cross.

Tell me about your Mom.

My mother grew up on a farm north of Gravelbourg, SK. She has been married to my Dad for about fourteen years and is a huge help around the farm. Whether it is making lunches for our staff, working in the office, or working with cattle, she does her job well. She volunteers with the community a lot, is on the board of our local Farm It Forward fund raiser committee and likes to joke she's Mossbank's most famous model.

Tell me about your Dad.

Dad grew up on the Lazy Y, and at age twenty, he started managing the operation, growing it to what we are today with my Mom and my grandparents. He enjoys the challenges that farming brings. Although Dad works hard, he always finds time to spend with the family and takes me hunting, snowmobiling, and dirt biking. He enjoys the outdoors and is constantly teaching me about life.

Describe a typical day after you get home from school? What do you do on a typical weekend?

I enjoy hunting and all things hunting-related. When I get home from school or have the day off, you can often find me hunting, spotting deer, checking trail cams, trying to find shedded antlers, dirt biking, or just enjoying the outdoors.

I'm constantly finding ways to expand my entrepreneurship. For example, a couple of summers ago, when we had a large surplus of gophers, I saw the opportunity to start a small game taxidermy business. I also started breeding rabbits. The latest business I've established is a magazine called "Everything Country Mag," which has been doing very well!

What kind of jobs do you have on your farm? How do you think your life differs from your friends who live in town?

My jobs around the farm vary by season. I'm helping out with the calving season from March to June -- helping to tag calves, bed pens, feeding and watering cows, etc. During harvest, I help service equipment in the morning, and I'm commonly on bin duty for the rest of the day. Bin duty means taking samples, helping truckers unload, cleaning bins, and being the general yard gopher to keep things running smoothly. I also help maintain the yard by cutting grass, tilling trees, etc.

I think my life differs from kids in the town primarily because I have more areas to play and explore. I feel fortunate to have a large yard and lots of roaming grounds to do most activities desired. I believe that another advantage of living on a farm is the opportunity to work with my family on the various jobs that come with farming. For example, on my farm, we have families from other countries who come to work as employees, fix equipment, do office work, herd cattle, and just about everything in between.

What is the thing you love most about living on a farm?

The freedom of it. There's so much you can do on a farm. I can dirt bike, hunt, walk around, breathe fresher air, and connect with the environment much better. Gravel and dirt are my preference over concrete, that's for sure!

How do you feel being raised on a farm helps to shape you and your future?

Being raised on the farm has shown me a strong work ethic, and it toughened me up a lot. I think I'll be a lot better off getting a job or having a business in the future. I've been exposed to many business transactions and a diverse group of people (you never know who is going to drive into the yard tomorrow). I live in the workplace and get to watch my parents manage a business. I get to explore the countryside, and I get a view beyond a screen.

If there was one key thing you wish non-farmers would know about farmers or farming - what do you wish it was?

I wish people realized that farmers are not the problem in this world. I think farmers get a bad rap. Industrial animal farmers get hit hard by animal rights activists, farmers near cities get it because they spray their crops, and so much more. I hope that someday we will come to an understanding with non-farmers so that we can feed them without fussing. At the end of the day, farmers are just caretakers.

Rianne Boekhorst, Manitoba

YEAR BORN: 1993

"KID FROM THE 90s/2000s"

Photo supplied.

Where did you grow up? How many siblings do you have?

I was born in the Netherlands and lived there until age thirteen. In 2006, we moved to a small town named Brunkild, south of Winnipeg, Manitoba. I have two brothers and a sister. I'm the oldest.

What kind of farm did you grow up on?

We have always had mixed farm operations. In the Netherlands, we had broilers, dairy, and a number of different crops, including canola, wheat, sugar beets, rye grass, black currants, potatoes, barley, and corn. In Canada, we grow wheat, rye grass, corn, soybeans, and canola and have about 50,000 laying hens.

What are the key memories and qualities that come up when you think of your Mom?

Caring. My Mom was and is the backbone of the farm operation. She is the person that is always there to support in case something doesn't go right.

"Can you pick up some parts?"
"We need another combine driver!"
"Can you bring the meals early because we need to change fields soon oh, and while you are there, we need your help with that too?"
"Mom, I'm sick. Can you pick me up from school?"
"Oh, Mom, my orthodontist appointment is today. When are you picking me up?"

Unfortunately, she is also the person that gets the least credit in our home. She is the one who brings the family together and brings the "family" part of family farming into our household. The key memory for me is that she was always there. If Mom could not be there, she would leave notes as to what we needed to do (before cell phones became popular), but it was always very strange when she wasn't there. When I was at an age where it was safe to let me cook, she would leave directions on how to make supper. She would have everything ready, and I would just have to put the food on the stove. I remember watching the food the whole time it was on the stove to make sure it didn't burn. I was so thankful when she came home, and she could finish off supper!

Tell me about your Dad.

My Dad spent a lot of time working on the farm. When we were young, we got to ride on farm equipment with him. Sometimes it was hard to sit still for that long, and my lunch kit would be empty much sooner than his, but I have great memories of going along for rides. He also taught all of us how to drive anything we needed to drive. Sometimes there was a bit of impatience on the "teaching" part, and we got to "learn as we went," but that was part of the fun. I never saw him sit and relax at home very much. He was there for meals, but we did family activities, mostly in the evenings and Sundays.

What was a typical day like for you after you got home from school? What do you remember doing most on the weekends?

There was always something to do, but this also depended on the time of year. After school, we did get all the time we needed to work on homework, but you just knew that if things were busy on the farm, we should do our homework on the bus ride home.

Depending on how old I was, there were chores I had to do after school. But overall, we always tried to try to eat dinner as a family, do our homework, and go to bed at a reasonable time.

I remember that Saturdays were always busy days. It was always the "extra" things that needed some attention. I remember being able to stay up a little later Saturday night if we did a good job helping. This was also the only evening we got to drink pop and have chips!

Sundays were typically more family focused. Depending on the time of year and how busy it was on the farm, we would go to the beach, park, have visitors over, or have a barbecue.

What would you say was a key activity you did to entertain yourself as a child? As a teen?

Although living more rural than most other kids, I never had a hard time entertaining myself. We built tunnels and forts out of straw bales and had a tire swing that we always came back to. Birthday parties at our house were simple, and I remember them being fun. For years, we played hide and seek in the machine shed. I was one of the few people that lived on a farm, so I had lots of people wanting to come over to the farm to play.

As a teen, it was mostly chores I did for entertainment. We had just moved to Canada, so there was lots of work to be done, and we didn't speak the language well to communicate with our classmates. We did a lot as a family. Part of that included exploring Manitoba, but a lot of time was spent building up our farm here. I think we appreciated our trips to the beach, or road trips to the United States even more because so much time was spent at home.

What did you like best about farming when you were younger?

When I was very young, I enjoyed the amount of space and freedom I had on the farm -- getting a super tall swing, riding bikes in the yard, and climbing bales -- all things that were less common for people in the city. We kept ourselves busy without technology!

Later, it was the idea of contributing to a common goal -- getting the crop off before the frost, combining until late at night, and being back early in the field in the morning. Many kids don't get to see exactly what their parents do. What does work as an accountant or engineer really look like? These are jobs you don't know the ins and outs of until you actually do them. I saw and lived a unique lifestyle every day and learned so much about the business. It's so unique, and by watching and being involved, I got to learn more than I ever comprehended at the time.

Did you feel brothers were treated differently than sisters in your family? Were expectations different?

I think there is a difference, but I believe this is a result of personal interests rather than a gender difference. I am the oldest, so I did farm-related chores because I was the most capable "kids farmhand" at the time. I also didn't mind it.

With both my brothers farming now, the opportunity to do the same things I did isn't there for my sister, who is the youngest one of all of us. I am certain that if she had the desire to be more involved on the farm, they would welcome her with open arms, but it has to come from both sides. It wasn't a given, nor more desired, that the boys were the ones who continued to farm, but they showed the most interest from an early age. Now that they have shown that interest, they take on many more farm responsibilities.

How do you feel being raised on a farm helped shape you and your future?

I didn't realize how many things I learned on the farm until I started working off-farm. Responsibility, work ethic, prioritizing, teamwork, communication, and it doesn't end there. Since you are immersed in a "farm business," it's almost like you've worked somewhere for your whole life, with some of the early childhood years as a "trainee," as I was watching my parents do it. Things that are common sense to farm-raised people are usually not to people outside the farm.

It gave me a head start for the future and allowed me to focus on things that I couldn't learn on the farm. It also changed my perspective on life. Issues for others weren't an issue for me. At times, this resulted in a somewhat harsh response from my end when talking to them (I'm working on developing that still), but sometimes I also had an out-of-the-box solution that solved their problem.

If there was one key thing you wish non-farmers would know about farmers or farming - what do you wish it was?

I wish people knew that farmers want the best for everyone. This includes their animals, the people, and the environment. If something farm-related doesn't look appealing or political, there's often a reason for it.

Wes Froese, Manitoba

Year born: 1957

"Kid from the 60s"

Wes, his wife Elaine, and their grandkids. Photo supplied.

Where did you grow up? How many siblings do you have?

I didn't grow up until later in life, my wife encouraged it. I had three older sisters who thought I was spoiled, but I would disagree. We grew up on a family farm near Boissevain, Manitoba, 45 minutes south of Brandon. I am the youngest.

What kind of farm did you grow up on?

We had cattle and grain with a seed cleaning plant. I had my first seed certificate when I was 12. My sisters and I worked in the fields driving tractor, baling, feeding, and chasing cows.

What are your key memories of your Mom?

My mom was a hard-working, amazing woman who was supportive to my dad. I worked alongside my mom many times, and it is her farm from her father that we now own. When I was younger, she milked the cows, fed the hired men, raised children, tended the garden, and supported the work of her husband who was also a church pastor.

Tell me about your Dad.

His first love was the church. I never saw him fix anything or grease anything. He always had help with the mechanical work. He could do physical work being a very strong man. He enjoyed the people end of things and was honest and well thought of in the community. He worked alongside his wife in decision making when it came to farm stuff. There were times that he would prepare sermons in the truck while waiting for the combines. Often, he would have his coveralls over his shirt and tie, as he was willing to drop his farm work to go to serve others in town or a church meeting. He rarely got paid for any church work and was very generous with his finances.

What was a typical day for you like after you got home from school?

In the busy seasons, I would have chores to be done with the cows and be expected to work in the fields. I couldn't play winter sports because I needed a ride. I did manage to play baseball because I could ride my bike to town which was three miles away. Dad held me back from driving everything and carrying 100 lb bags. I always was trying to push my limits and Dad made sure that I did not get in over my head.

What do you remember doing most on the weekends?

Chores and going to church. Playing, working, having people over, sometimes going to Lake William to swim. When I was older, I played baseball every weekend and lots of high school sports. I started combining when I was 12.

What is the biggest way you think farming has changed in your lifetime?

The biggest change is that there was no money to be had except the absolute basics. Today we have more money, and everything is so expensive. There is so much less physical work, we don't even have to steer! Armstrong steering is over now that we have autosteer.

What did you like best about farming when you were younger?

I liked doing the physical work and driving things and being outside. I liked the challenge of doing things and seeing what I accomplished. With farming you can usually see what you have done at the end of the day.,

What do you think we as farmers are doing well now?

I think we are providing safe, inexpensive food for consumers.

What kind of things do you wish we were doing more of?

I wish we were working together and helping each other more. We used to work together as neighbours more.

Faber Girls, Washington, USA

Lily, Age 5/ Addie, Age 7/ Leyla, Age 9

"Kids from Today"

Photo supplied.

What kind of farm do you live on, and where is it located?

We live on a cow farm in Washington.

What is the best part of living on a farm?

Lily: Going to the sand and food piles at the farm.

Addie: We can run in the fields and jump on haybales.

Leyla: We get to work with the cows.

Tell me the best thing about your Mom.

Lily: She hugs me.

Addie: She loves me and takes care of me.

Leyla: She lets us have sweets.

What is the coolest thing about your Dad?

Lily: He goes really fast on boats.

Addie: He gets us lots of sweets and is funny.

Leyla: He owns a farm in Oregon.

Have any pets?

Yes, we have two cats and one dog.

Leyla: I had three other cats, but they got eaten by coyotes.

What is the coolest machine on your farm?

Lily: Trucks that carry cow food.

Addie: The manure scrapper tractor.

Leyla: The corn chopper

What do you want to be when you grow up?

Lily: A doctor.

Addie: A horse rider.

Leyla: A Vet.

"Life with Lily" – by "Dad," Dwayne Faber

While helping feed cows, Lily told me she was going to share her coke with a cow and promptly offered her straw to a cow.

"Life with Addie" – by "Dad," Dwayne Faber

Addie: Can I have a horse?
Dad: No, horses don't make any money.
Addie, after a few moments: But you say cows don't make any money either.

"Life with Leyla" – by "Dad," Dwayne Faber

While driving between farms, Leyla asked if I was the boss. I said yes, and asked what the boss did, with excitement at her response. She replied: "The boss doesn't do anything; they just drive around."

Amy VanderHeide, Nova Scotia

Year born: 1986

Kid from the 90s

Photo supplied.

Where did you grow up? How many siblings do you have?

I grew up in the small community of Prospect, Nova Scotia. I was fortunate to live in an area that overlooked the beautiful farmland of the Annapolis Valley.

I love where I grew up. My younger brother and I were surrounded by family. We lived next door to our grandmother on one side, and our aunt and a cousin, who we joke is our "other brother" because we all spent so much time with each other on the other side. I am so thankful for that as we remain close to this day.

My brother stayed close to the house we grew up in and lives just a few doors down with my nephew. My parents are still in the same place as well.

Our roots run deep. Our grandparents were one of the first families to make their homes there, and I am thankful to have that home base to return to. Even though I am only a few minutes away, and my brother is even closer, we still refer to it as home.

What kind of farm did you grow up on?

I grew up one generation removed from the family farm. However, since my grandmother lived next door and the cow-calf farm was there, I always say I grew up on the farm raising beef cattle. Even though my Mom didn't stay on the farm, my grandmother's farm was the central hub for the family.

Every fall, the whole family, farmers or not, would help to bring the cattle home from pasture and pitch in however needed. My Dad can tell a few stories of things he's helped with since he began dating my Mom and from their marriage. It was definitely a family-run farm, and everyone was there when needed, whether helping with the cattle or during fencing and hay seasons.

Even growing up, Sunday dinners were held at my grandmother's. I don't know exactly what age I was when that petered out; however, I remember those dinners vividly, and they are treasured memories.

What was a typical day like for you after you got home from school? What do you remember doing most on the weekends?

The school bus stopped at my grandmother's house, in the barnyard, to be exact. Our grandmother was our primary babysitter, so we'd often have homemade cookies, pie, or another homemade treat as soon as we got in the house. We used to drop our bags and head straight to the laundry room, which is where she used to lay out everything she had baked that day. She still does!

In middle school and high school, I would often get up before school to help my aunts and uncle do chores, and I would repeat that in the evening. At the time, our cows were kept in stanchions. We fed and cleaned them twice a day, and during calving, would check barns multiple times a day and move the cows from their stanchions into a maternity pen as needed.

I remember my barely five feet tall grandmother lugging newborn calves on feed sacks or in the calf sled we had at the time, into pens with these big Hereford cows following along behind her. She never seemed to think twice that the cow may not have appreciated that so much. She just did it anyway.

The weekends were very much the same. As I got older, I could do checks on my own and could start chores before the others arrived. During busier times, I would help with vaccinating, making hay and other jobs that popped up.

Once in high school, I got a job and wasn't there as much on the weekends, but I could always pitch in whenever possible. I was always happiest on the farm, even then.

What would you say was a key activity you did to entertain yourself as a child? As a teen?

My brother, cousin, and I were always together as children. My cousin and I are two months apart to the day (he's older). That two months is a lot when you're kids, so that led to lots of competition between us, who could whistle first, snap their fingers, ride their bike and who was the toughest, the most common. I still say I won that every time.

We may have been known to have a fistfight or two when things got out of hand. We worked it all out in the end! Most of that happened at my grandmother's since we were all there before and after school. I can still hear her threats to call my aunts, who would show up to put us in our place if necessary. The three us together could do a lot of cool things, but we could also be the perfect storm. All things we laugh about when we are together now.

When we weren't competing, we built forts in the trees and my grandmother's old duck house that was falling down. She wouldn't let us play in it, but we snuck in as often as possible to grab old boards to use them for forts. We also built jumps for our bikes and would race around her yard for hours.

We also helped her with chores. Often, we'd arrive to a pile of wood to haul or buckets of maple sap to be carried into the house for her to make syrup.

Sometimes we would help collect eggs, but she was particular about her chickens and didn't want us in there getting them over-excited or scared (which only made us want to be in there even more.)

As a teen, I got more into sports. I played volleyball almost through high school. Once I got my license, I had a weekend job at Oaklawn Farm Zoo during the school year and worked at a farm market after school. I met my now husband when I was 16, so between my jobs and spending time with him on his farm, I didn't have much free time. By now, the farm had started a transition of sorts as my aunt and uncle started taking over and changing how it operated, so there wasn't as much to do as the cows didn't require as many hands on. Something that was better for us and the cattle as well.

I wasn't someone who loved school, and I was able to collect the required credits and finish my grade 12 year in January. At 18, I started doing data entry at our local poultry plant, where my Dad was the Vice President. Eventually, I worked my way into maintenance and inventory clerking and filled in working in the accounts receivable and payable departments.

Office positions were not my happy place either. When I married my husband at age 19, I started working as a horticulture research assistant for my aunt's agriservices business, and after our first son was born a few years later, I stayed on the farm full-time.

What is something about your Mom's parenting that you appreciate so much more now that you're grown?

Mom never got worked up over the small things, was never a helicopter parent, and didn't ever pressure us to do more than our best. She and my Dad were also very open with us, especially as teenagers. No topic was off topic, which made our dinner conversations interesting!

Now that I am a mom, I can appreciate those things and am much more laid back because of it. We are open with our kids about things and talk to them about everything. I wasn't sheltered from things, so it paved the way for me to be the same with my own children.

I see my Mom in a lot of what I do as a parent, and it's given me so much more appreciation for what she did for us as kids. It still does to this day!

Tell me about your Dad.

I don't know if I've ever told my Dad how much of a hero he is to me.

While I was growing up, my Dad worked his way up from a truck driver for a local processing plant to being the VP. He went to night school, travelled for courses and for work with a processing plant out-of-province. So, he was often gone a week or more at a time.

It was busy, and a lot of work for my Mom at home with my brother and me, and a full-time job, while he was gone. However, I don't really remember much about him not being home because he always made up for it.

When he was home, he was home. We went camping, spent time as a family unit and travelled. He was busy and had a stressful career, but he did it all for us. He never wanted any of us to want for anything, but he also made sure we knew the value of hard work.

We always did our firewood as a family; he took us with him snowplowing and he gave us jobs and chores to do. If he was working on something, he often had one or both of us at his side so we could learn how to do what he was doing.

My Dad is also full of stories and life experiences, and he has used all of them to teach us a lesson in one way or another.

My parents are both young, in their mid-50s, and working full-time jobs. My Dad has had some major health challenges that were scary for us as a family, and even during those times, he was most concerned for us.

Dad always did and still does want the best for our families and us. He gave us the greatest example by working incredibly hard for everything we have.

We share a lot of similarities, even though people often compare me to my mother first, and I really treasure those comparisons even when they may not be flattering.

We are both stubborn, have our own ideas on things, and are often opinionated. We're also both quietly smart (a lot of what goes through our brains is never shared), forward-thinking and natural leaders. All of these things make us a powerful team, and maybe sometimes fierce opposition.

He's also very private, sometimes secretive, and often happiest when he's home and not out in public or surrounded by people. He is the type of person who puts forward a tough exterior, but on the inside loves to cuddle kittens and is also the first person our family calls when we need help with something. (I can hear the reaction he'll have when he eventually reads that line, but it's true!)

He's also probably wishing I didn't share any of this with so many people, but inside he's humbled and may even shed a tear when no one is looking.

He's someone I've always looked up to, even if I haven't been as open as I could be with him.

The examples of hard work, determination and perseverance have been key components that have shaped me into the person I am today. While both of my parents have been role models for me, my Dad is more so the one I've looked up to in certain areas of my life. Such as when it comes to expanding my career to roles off the farm and having the backbone it sometimes takes to become a leader.

What did you like best about your farming experience when you were younger?

Thinking back on my younger years on the farm, the thing I liked the best was how it brought us all together. As I mentioned before, when we all came together, even as young kids, to bring the cattle home, or for Sunday dinners. That time together to me is something that I look back on with the greatest fondness.

Did you feel girls and boys were treated differently in your family while growing up? Were expectations different?

Not at all. Partly because of my grandfather's passing the year I was born; however, it started long before that. He and my grandmother had four girls and one boy. My aunts worked on the farm long after my uncle, who was the oldest of the brood, moved out and took on his own career. Then after my grandfather passed away, it was them and my grandmother who did the day-to-day running of the farm. They had help, a hired hand who would help do chores since they were still in high school and college, and family would all pitch in when needed. They didn't do it alone, but they didn't feel like they needed a man there to lead them.

The only clear "gender role" I think of was that of my grandmother. She cooked and baked for everyone and still does; she cleaned, kept everyone clothed, made family and church priorities and above all, she kept the house running and everyone in order. That being said, she enjoyed all of that, and it wasn't a role she was forced in because she was a woman.

When my grandfather passed away, it didn't become a question as to if she could or would keep the farm going, she just did.

My grandma's kids had been taught jobs based on their ability, not their gender, so there were no considerable gaps to fill or questions they couldn't answer and, therefore, they could carry on because they were all treated and taught equally.

The same was true in our household growing up. My Dad taught me everything he also taught my brother and maybe, in some instances, made sure to teach me because I was a female. He was always very hands-on in teaching us when he was working on vehicles or teaching us to drive, but also in planning for the future, doing a budget or helping us make financial decisions.

I am lucky to have grown up the way I did, especially in the farming community. I think my life and my family were a bit unique, and I am so thankful for that. Although it could have given me an unrealistic view of the world, I think it better prepared me for life and standing up for myself in a male-dominated industry.

How do you feel being raised on a farm helped shape you and your future?

I think being raised on a farm shaped me as a person who understands life. Being raised on a farm means we are witness to the cycles of life from such an early age. I think it develops an intense awareness of things around you. The changes in nature, the relationship with the earth and how all of that is so important to the day-to-day life on the farm.

I think beyond making me strong, resilient, and proud, it also shaped me into someone who can be flexible, understanding, empathetic and thoughtful. And, of course, respectful. If we don't respect our environment, no matter what we do with our lives and environment, we won't get the most out of it.

I would say being raised on a farm, or even in a farm family, taught me to keep things simple, to work hard, and that a bit of stubbornness will take you a long way.

If there was one key thing you wish non-farmers knew about farmers or farming, what do you wish it was?

I want non-farmers to know that farmers do the very best they can to bring food to your table. More than corporations, we are family farms and want the same thing for our family, as you do for yours.

There is so much more that goes into growing food, whether it's animal, vegetable, fruit, grains, and I'd really encourage people to connect with farmers and learn from us first. We want to tell our story, and we want people to get to know us so they can be assured that we take growing food seriously.

We share a lot of the same values, and our families top that list. Farmers and non-farmers alike are striving to put the best, safest, healthiest, and most responsibly grown food on our tables. Any chance farmers can get to talk with non-farmers about that shared value, we'll take!

Edith Paul, Alberta

Year born: 1929

"Kid from the 30s"

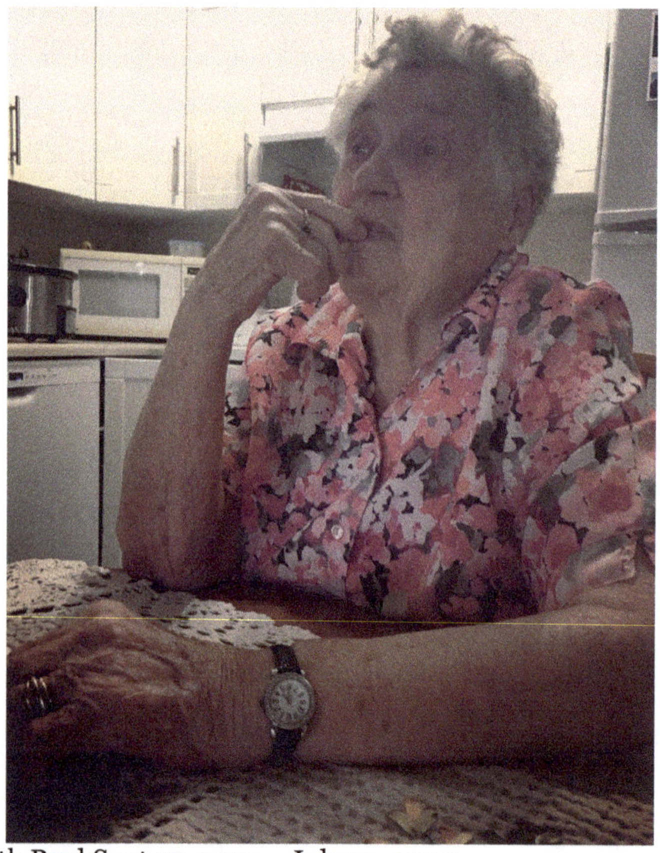

Edith Paul Sept 17, 1929 – July 15, 2020.
Photo by: Billi J. Miller

Where did you grow up? How many siblings do you have?

I grew up in the Thomasville District, near Lloydminster, Alberta. I had three brothers and one sister that passed away as an infant.

What kind of farm did you grow up on?

We farmed grain and had cattle, chickens, and pigs.

What are your key memories of your Mom?

My mom worked hard. My dad was killed by a horse when I was in my early teens. She loved to garden. She had a good heart. She baked the best bread.

Tell me about your Dad.

Dad was a good singer, and he had a beautiful voice. He went to church on Sundays. Sundays were for rest, even for the horses. No cards on Sundays.

What was a typical day for you like after you got home from school?

I went to school until grade nine. On our way home, we filled the water tank and came home to do chores.

What do you remember doing most on weekends?

Ball games, church on Sunday, picnics, chores. I didn't do machinery, but I did all the same work my brothers did. I stooked, and I loved thrashing.

I left the farm at 20.

What is the biggest way you think farming has changed in your lifetime?

It's become more mental work than physical work. We worked with our hands; now they must work with their heads. Long hours are the same.

What did you like about farming when you were younger?

I loved all the farm work, but thrashing was my favourite time. We had breaks between seasons; that's also something that's changed.

What do you think we, as farmers, are doing well now?

You work hard, but you need to figure out a way to take more breaks.

What kind of things do you wish we were doing more of?

I think you're moving too fast.

Tracy Desmarais, Alberta

Year born: 1974

Kid from the 80s

Photo by: Billi J. Miller

Where did you grow up? How many siblings do you have?

I grew up on a farm about five minutes north of Paradise Valley, in east-central Alberta (AB). I have three siblings – two brothers and one sister.

What kind of farm did you grow up on?

We were grain and pig farmers (farrow to finish). We had about 130 sows.

What is something about your Mom's parenting that you appreciate more now that you're grown?

So many good things! My Mom worked very hard every day in the barns, and during seeding and harvest, she worked extra hard because she still had the pigs every day, plus helping in the fields. She always fit everything in, even if she started at 4 a.m. She had an outstanding work ethic. She also got us to all our sporting events and activities. She made everything "family" important!

Tell me about your Dad.

My Dad worked hard! If he wasn't driving a combine, seeder, or truck, he was welding, fixing, or machining in the shop. He also did all the fixing and maintenance in the barns. I learned so much from working alongside him that I still use now. One thing I remember him saying a lot was, "Do I need to put up a post to make sure you are moving?" I find myself saying that to my kids every now and then. As busy as my Dad was, he always made time to be at our sporting and school events. I really respect him for that!

What was a typical day like for you after you got home from school? What do you remember doing most on the weekends?

Some mornings before school, I had to do chores in the barns. After school, I had horses, so I would usually go riding, and depending on what sport I was playing at the time, I was either playing or training for them. I also had to make a lot of meals as Mom worked in the barns a lot. During harvest, it was straight out to the fields to help one way or the other.

What would you say was a key activity you did to entertain yourself as a child? As a teen?

I rode horses a lot. But, between my horses and sports, I didn't have much time for anything else extracurricular. We were lucky to have quads, bikes, and sleds to keep us busy, too.

What did you like best about farming when you were younger?

There was lots of freedom to do and have what other kids didn't. We were fortunate to have the ability to do sports and have horses, quads, and sleds to ride. Our parents trusted us to be off and do whatever we wanted because we were responsible. Don't get me wrong – we still got into trouble for pushing limits.

Did you feel girls and boys were treated differently in your family while growing up? Were expectations different?

My older brother and I were treated the same; we both had chores to do. The expectations were the same. My younger brother also helped around the farm as he got older. The only difference was probably that I did a lot of the cooking at times.

How do you feel being raised on a farm helped shape you and your future?

Being raised on a farm greatly impacted my priorities and work ethic as I got older. Growing up on a farm gave me many advantages with life skills that are so important to me that I pass on to my kids. We were raised with high respect for our parents, neighbours, co-workers, and "things."

If there was one key thing you wish non-farmers knew about farmers or farming – what would it be?

I wish people who don't farm could see how flexible and self-sufficient farmers are. They are truck drivers, welders, mechanics, vets, problem-solvers, equipment operators, volunteers, and doctors. Our families come first, and if anyone is in need, they are treated like family.

Max Merrild, Alberta

Year born: 2015

"Kid from today"

Photo by: Billi J. Miller

What kind of farm do you live on?

Grain.

Do you have brothers or sisters?

Two brothers, Martin, and Magnus and one sister, Sophia.

Tell me the best thing about your Mom.

Probably that she goes to town and gets lots of groceries.

What is the coolest thing about your Dad?

He takes me for rides in the combine.

Have any pets?

Two little kitties named Fluffy and Frank. A dog named Guinness.

What's the coolest machine on your farm?

Oh, our Challenger tractor. We bought it last year, and it's so big! It is a 4-wheel drive with duals.

What do you want to be when you grow up?

A grain farmer.

What do you think it would be like to live in the city?

Hmmm, not really good. It's just house to house to house to house with so many people. My favourite part of living on the farm is working in the shop.

Elaine Froese, Manitoba

Year born: 1956

"Kid FROM the 60s"

Photo supplied.

Where did you grow up? How many siblings do you have?

I grew up on the first farm east of Winnipeg, Manitoba, near Dugald, only 15 minutes from Portage and Main.

I had the best of both worlds, chasing cows, driving a combine, and going to the theatre in Winnipeg. I am the oldest of five children and the fourth generation of farm kids.

My younger brother is farming the family farm today near Dugald. I have been married to Wes Froese for 40 years, farming near Boissevain, Manitoba as a farm partner. We are now transitioning our seed business to our son and daughter-in-law.

What kind of farm did you grow up on?

Our farm was mixed with a cow/calf operation which became a feedlot. Our house was known as the "help house" since it was built in 1907 by my great-grandfather Peter Lindsay Edie who bought land from a Métis woman. We often helped folks who had car trouble or got stuck along Dugald Road. We also chased a lot of steers as young kids. My Mom took a lot of pride in the yard's landscaping and always ensured that everyone was well-fed with fresh garden produce, grass-fed beef, and home preserves.

What are your key memories of your Mom?

My Mom was a strong woman who expected to be treated as an equal partner in the farm business. She served in many roles outside the farm to help farm families, like the Women's Institute (as president of the province), Manitoba Farm Vacations, Adult

Learning, and the Beef Information Centre. She was very interested in agricultural policy and was a lifetime director of the Western Canadian Wheat Growers. She was a woman of quiet faith who raised five children, four of whom are entrepreneurs, and one who was killed at age 23 by a drunk driver.

She taught us to be leaders with a voice, contribute to the community, observe, examine, and compare. She wanted me to be a lawyer, but I think she was happy that I used my communication skills in other ways. My Mom was awarded the 150 Trailblazer Award for Manitoba, as was I. Unfortunately, she died young, at 65, with an asthma attack during harvest.

Tell me about your Dad.

My Dad was the oldest of six, mothered by a teacher and a dairy farm dad fifteen years older. He left his family farm to be on his own as a young married man, worked very hard with Hereford cattle, and then steers in a feedlot. He and Mom were the Red River Exhibition Farm Family of the Year in 1974 when wheat was a great price, and he had just built two Harvestore silos, the first ones in Manitoba. Like my Mom, he also went to many meetings for the Cattleman's Association, KAP, Crop Insurance, Manitoba Ag Hall of Fame, and other groups. He also loved to dance and called square dances, which I attended at a young age. He was known as a "gentle giant" by local neighbours, who knew they could count on his help. He was happy to let me watch him calf out the Herefords. Dad also said that I could do anything I put my mind to. He was talented with public speaking, as was my Mom, and encouraged my involvement in 4-H.

What was a typical day for you like after you got home from school?

As the oldest, I likely did what was requested after I finished my homework. I was encouraged to do art, folk dance, highland dancing, and piano, so we had many chances to grow and do sports after school. The coaches from our school would give us rides home as we lived on the main highway. I don't recall doing a lot of farm chores, mostly things Mom needed in the house and garden or mowing the lawn. We did have TV, and I remember watching Hogan's Heroes, which was my brother's choice. We also loved Walt Disney on Sunday nights. I took piano lessons but preferred dancing and singing in the choir. I spent many summers as a camp kitchen helper or camp counsellor, which allowed great freedom to learn leadership at Camp Wannakumbac and Camp Arnes.

What do you remember doing most on the weekends?

As a teen, I was busy playing high school sports and learning to drive in Winnipeg. Dad taught me how to operate the combine, and we also stacked square bales, which we also enjoyed as mega straw forts. I sometimes rode my pony, and we would go tobogganing on the slopes of the Floodway, which carved out some of our land in the 1960s. Dad would also take us skating at Dugald where the barrel stove warmed the skates, and we swam lots in the summer at the Oasis. Our cousins lived close by, and we played a lot of football and hide and seek with flashlights.

What is the biggest way you think farming has changed in your lifetime?

The innovations in technology, having a computer to do records and drive automatic functions are the most amazing. I grew up without videos, microwaves, cell phones, and computers. All of those things are part of my daily routine now. The strong work ethic continues, and the risks of nature and pricing remain. We reap what we sow, but unless God blesses the crops with rain -- nothing grows.

What did you like best about farming when you were younger?

Being able to do many different things in different seasons and be in charge of your plans for the day. I think the strong ag-political leanings of my parents encouraged me to have a voice for change and consider that change is inevitable, but growth is optional. I really enjoyed all the great play times we could have in the pasture with forts, straw bale forts, and snow houses. We spent a lot of time creating our own fun, and my Mom was not constraining our adventures, even rafting in a full ditch of cold water.

What do you think we as farmers are doing well now?

I think farmers are doing a great job of land stewardship, efficient production and seeking innovation. There is always room for improvement on the people side of things, as communication in farm families is a key issue I deal with in my coaching practice. Many farms have a great culture, as my family of origin did in some ways, yet my parents had weaknesses in how they transitioned the farm. My in-laws did a great job of their transition, so I have seen a full spectrum of stories.

What kind of things do you wish we were doing more of?

Talking and listening with empathy and curiosity. If farm families would work on their value alignment, treat each other with better behaviour, and have collaborative decision-making between generations, all of agriculture would benefit from a stronger farm family culture.

We all get to choose how we show up to lead our farm teams, treat others with respect, and give everyone on the team a respected voice that counts. I like to challenge the current mindsets that may need shifting. I likely got a good grounding in this approach with my Irish DNA and participating in the Springfield Youth Parliament where I was the first female premier.

I also wish farm families would work on more self-awareness to grow as life-long learners. Doing conflict resolution well is a great skill for navigating life and can be learned. Communicating well will help farm families transition in a way that secures the legacy of the farm and family for generations. I wish that for all farm families.

Vernon Marlatt, Saskatchewan

Year born: 1922

"Kid in the 30s"

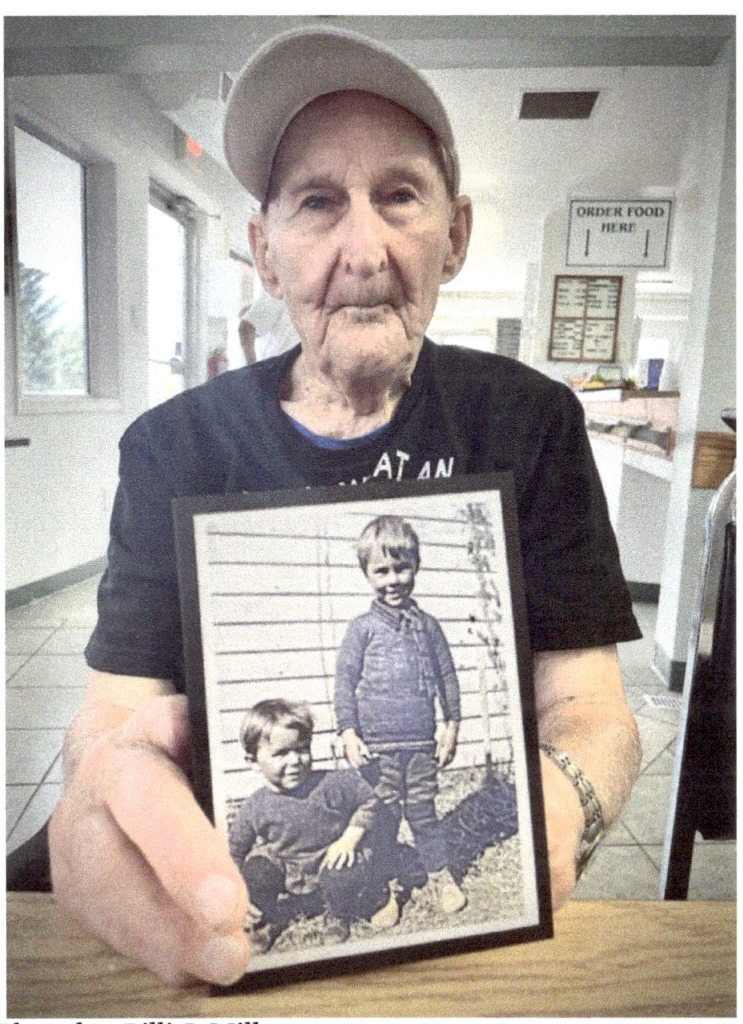

Photo by: Billi J. Miller

Where did you grow up? How many siblings do you have?

I grew up on a farm outside of Lashburn, Saskatchewan with my two brothers, Don and Gordon, and one sister, Jean.

What kind of farm did you grow up on?

A mixed farm. We had everything from cows to chickens, horses, pigs, turkeys, and grain.

What are your key memories of your Mom?

Mom was a hardworking lady. She was a home keeper who could do anything and everything. She would help anyone if needed. She was a great lady. She died at 102.

Tell me about your Dad.

Dad was also a very hard-working man. He was a good farm manager, who was very quiet and gentle. Helped each of us kids get set up in life. He passed away at 78 of cancer.

What was a typical day for you like after you got home from school?

Came home and milked cows, weeded garden, brought horses in, and filled the wood box.

What do you remember doing most on the weekends?

In the summer, we went stooking, picking berries, and we went up the hill to the pasture and played softball with all the neighbours, and we made a team. The odd

Saturday, we would get a nickel and we got to go to town for either a chocolate bar, ice cream, or Johnny cakes and Roger's corn syrup. Weekends were also a time when we would go visit family.

What is the biggest way you think farming has changed in your lifetime?

I came from doing our farm work with horses. Nowadays the farm machinery can do more in an hour than what we could do in a week.

What did you like best about farming when you were younger?

At the time I liked everything about it. I really enjoyed farming because I didn't know any different.

What do you think we as farmers are doing well now?

Managing the land better.

What kind of things do you wish we were doing more of?

Living off the land more. More gardening, pigs, chickens, etc.

Madeline Miller, Alberta

Year born: 2011

"Kid from today"

Photo by: Billi J. Miller

What kind of farm do you live on?

A grain and cattle farm.

What is the best part of living on a farm?

The freedom.

Tell me the best thing about your Mom.

That she made me a person and she takes care of us.

What is the coolest thing about your Dad?

That he's a farmer, and his whole family has been farming in Canada for 111 years.

Have any pets?

A Bernese Mountain dog named Bubbles Star Miller. Four cats: Cheese Waffles Miller, Wink Hamburger Miller, Shadow Blackie Miller, and Fluffy Polo Miller.

What's the coolest machine on your farm?

Our grain dryer. It's cool how it runs.

What do you want to be when you grow up?

I want to be a farmer and a teacher. At least a farmer. I want about fifty cows, one horse, a dog. I will calve the cows out and make my money that way. I'd also like one or two bulls.

One last thing, what do you think it would be like to live in the city?

There would be too much vehicle honking, and there would be too much noise, and you wouldn't be able to see any cows right outside your room window and you wouldn't be able to wake up to that beautiful sound of birds chirping and cows mooing. AND you wouldn't be able to smell the smell of silage.

"Life with Madeline" – by "Mom," Billi J. Miller

During the pandemic, I overheard the girls playing a game of "Would you Rather?"

Kate: "Madeline, would you rather live in an oven that's turned on, or a sink?"

Madeline (no hesitation): "Stove!"

Madeline to her Dad, age 4:

Sitting at the dinner table while Madeline looks at the newspaper, next Madeline says to her Dad:

"Dad, you gotta get off your wallet, because I need that bike."

Draw your family or your farm.

Image: Madeline Miller, Age 10

Jacquelyn Davidson, Alberta

Year born: 1995

Kid from the 2000s

Photo supplied.

Where did you grow up? How many siblings do you have?

I grew up on a small farm outside of Paradise Valley, Alberta. For those who don't know where that is, it's a piece of heaven on earth that I get to call home.

I have two younger sisters.

What kind of farm did you grow up on?

I grew up on a mixed cattle and grain farm. It is small but takes up so much of my heart. You can take me off the farm, but I have farm blood running through my veins.

What key memories and qualities come to mind when you think of your Mom?

Kindness. A servant's heart. She loves baking for others (she's famous for her brownies, BUT all of her baking is amazing). Family is important to her. She always tried to make it to all of our sporting events. She often cannot say no, so she always volunteers for something in the community or church out of love. She had a way of always lifting me when I was feeling down. When I was very young, she read to me every night and rubbed my back.

Tell me about your Dad.

My best friend. One of the hardest-working men I know, with a full-time job and a farm. He is very wise. He loves hockey (he still plays recreational hockey with the guys). Ever since I could walk, I have been his shadow. He was always there for me whenever I needed to talk.

He's easy-tempered and does not get stressed very easily. However, I am much like him, and we bottle things up. He is a fighter. He's had a few health scares; even in those times, he did not worry about the farm. I think he knew that his Mom (Grandma Davidson) would do enough worrying for the whole family.

What was a typical day like for you after you got home from school? What do you remember doing most on the weekends?

No matter what day of the week, I would always be outside (mostly so I did not have to do housework like cleaning, cooking, and baking).

On school days, my days would consist of homework. I would often cry because I never understood English or Social Studies._From a very young age, school was not easy for me. However, I was a hands-on learner. That's just one reason farming was so simple for me as Dad took the time and showed me what we were doing, and then he would explain it.

Next, my school days would mean chores, mainly working with the cows. After that, I was outside doing anything and everything. Often, I would be skidooing in the winter, and exploring around the farm, just because. I had track and field practice three times a week. I would help at AWANA or go to Bible study. Once I got my driver's license, I was the driver. My Mom loved that.

Harvest time meant I would run off the school bus to get on the combine.

On weekends, I was my Dad's right-hand on the farm. My duties included coffee with the farmers at the garage, going to the dump, avoiding housework from

Mom, or going to the grain elevator. I took part in a Youth group on Friday nights (from seventh grade and up). I was involved in track meets (year-round competitions). Afternoon skidoo rides. Church on Sundays.

Where do you see your adult life taking you?

Well, I hope to stay in the agriculture field somewhere, but God only knows. I also love traveling, and like my mother, I also have a servant's heart, so I love helping people where I can.

What are your best memories of being a farm kid?

Where do I begin? Everything I take for granted: the stars, the quiet, the open space, the neighbours!!! Learning to drive the truck on Dad's knee, my Dad being nervous about sending me to Kindergarten because of the calving stories I could have told, filling your boots while puddle jumping. Baby calves in the spring -- milksops that steal your heart -- bale jumping, mud bogging and skidooing. Talking with the guys about everything farming, trucks, skidoos.

COMBINING!!! (If you do not know me, I live to drive the combine in harvest).

The only time I got to skip school and stay home was to combine. I never thought it was fair that the boys got to skip school and combine all day. The lifestyle.

Did/do you feel pressure to farm as a farm kid?

Did I feel pressure to help on the farm? Yes, being the oldest and not having any brothers.

Calving/Seeding/Income Tax was always around the same time every year. Mom is a bookkeeper out of the house, so sometimes, she was stressed at that time of year. Dad seemed to always be more relaxed when seeding rolled around. The last few years, harvest has been crazy, and I have felt the pressure to help Dad get the crop off even though I was working off the farm.

However, both of my parents said that I needed to go to school past high school. I was not a fan, so I went to school for farming. But I never felt pressure from my Mom to farm. To my Dad, I think it was always something that I think he would love, but he knows the struggles of expanding the farm.

I did feel pressure from my Grandmother to farm.

Would I love to farm full-time? YES, 100 per cent. Can I do that full-time on my family farm? No. I would need a job off the farm and a ton of cash, as farming is a costly business to just start-up.

How do you feel being raised on a farm helped shape you and your future?

Farming has been my whole world and will always be a part of me wherever I go. It gives you a good work ethic -- you don't quit until the job is done. If you see something broken/wrong, your natural instinct is to fix it, or find a solution. You can talk about farming and the weather anywhere you go. Remember that someone is always worse off. Thank God for the things you do have and roll with the punches.

If there was one key thing you wish non-farmers would know about farmers or farming - what would that be?

Farmers have the best interest of their animals and land at heart. They work extremely hard for what they have because it's their life, not just their job. We work until the job or task is done, not just until 5 o'clock, and if we cannot finish it today, you know we'll be doing it again tomorrow.

Carys Purser, Alberta

Year born: 2010

"Kid from Today"

Photo supplied.

What kind of farm do you live on?

Cows, dogs and cats and a couple of crops. So, a cattle and grain farm.

What is the best part of living on a farm?

Being able to check cows.

Tell me the best thing about your Mom.

She gives us food. She makes food when we're harvesting. Takes good care of us when we're sick.

What's the coolest thing about your dad?

He's willing to help Grampa at work when he needs it.

Have any pets?

Cally, the grumpy cat. Fred, the dog. A calf named Bunter. Taffy, the girl kitten. Toby, the boy kitten.

What's the coolest machine on your farm?

The seeder.

What do you want to be when you grow up?

A vet.

Jean Hunter, Saskatchewan

Year born: 1921

"Kid from the 20s and 30s"

Photo supplied.

Where did you grow up? How many siblings do you have?

I grew up on our family farm in southeast Saskatchewan (SK), Canada, with two brothers, John and Norman, and two sisters, Jessie and Eva. Jessie grew up with a foster family in Weyburn, SK, where she was born. Our nearest neighbour was a half mile south over the prairie.

What kind of farm did you grow up on?

My Dad had dreams of a herd of Registered Red Poll cattle – a hornless breed but plans changed with the hardship of a few drought years. We had pigs, chickens, and sheep for a while. We tried to have turkeys once. My sister was given a set of turkey eggs for helping a neighbor a few days, but only one egg hatched.

I had two cats for playmates. One was a big tabby cat. I would run and hide, and he would always come and find me. The other was a mouser who always caught gophers and brought them to the doorstep.

I had a calf in the calf club, and after our field day, we had to take it down to the stockyard to ship it to Brandon, Manitoba. Three of us girls sat on the top rail crying as we said goodbye.

What are your key memories of your Mom?

My Mom had a world of patience. Dad thought nothing of coming home from town with extra people for supper at the last minute with the expectation that she just get out more plates and serve. I'm sure she never received the thanks she should have. She loved plants, and our house windowsills were full. Everything grew for her. She read a lot of books to me when I was little.

Tell me about your Dad.

Dad was definitely the boss. He knew how to whistle and had a special (two longs and two shorts) that was a signal we should show up to the call.

He sang, and he played our pump organ sometimes. He had a hymn book he had brought from Scotland – it was written not with notes, but doh, ray, me, fah setting. He was the Secretary Treasurer of our Municipality for nearly twenty-five years.

He was also a Justice of the Peace, so we saw the Royal Canadian Mounted Police (RCMP) quite often. He was fifty-seven when he passed away following surgery in Regina (the operation was successful, but the patient died).

What was a typical day for you like after you got home from school?

When I started school, we went by horse and buggy two and a half miles. During busy times, we walked to school because the horses were all busy in the fields with seeders, binders, and harrows (as they were horse-drawn).

Our little country school was only grades one through eight. Our teacher had to keep the fire going in a big pot-bellied heater for heat. Water was brought each day in a cream can for washing. Later, we'd get a furnace with registers, and indoor toilets would come too.

Our sports equipment was two bats and one softball. We never really had enough players for a ball team, though. We played a lot of other games, and the teacher played too. We would have field days in a nearby town, Alida, where we would compete for ribbons.

We always had a Christmas concert but not always a tree. We had carols, recitals, and two skits. We always had a Santa, and he would give us each a Christmas orange and a bit of hard candy. For grade nine, I went to Alida. We got our lessons from a correspondence school in Regina, so we depended on the mail. I did this for grades nine, ten and eleven.

We had dances in the school on Friday nights every two weeks during winter. There were three older bachelors who always asked us young girls to dance. My mother's rules were – we had to dance with them at least once, then we could make a case if we didn't want to dance when they asked again.

There were no telephones at school. One day at noon, a counsellor came on horseback to tell the teacher to dismiss school. There was a dust storm coming, and if we hurried, we may all make it home before it hit. We got home in time to find mother trying to get all the baby chicks safely into the five coops around the yard.

We always had a snack before chores. We collected eggs, took kitchen peelings to the pigs, brought in wood for the big wood box which was behind the kitchen stove.

What do you remember doing most on weekends?

On Saturday night, everyone was cleaned up, and we went to Carnduff. The whole neighbourhood was there. Carnduff was our main shopping centre for new clothes or shoes or groceries. The Salvation Army Band always came from Estevan and played and sang on one street corner.

Then, Sunday was a cleaning day. My sister and I took turns. One day I would have the upstairs to mop and dust, and she had the downstairs. The next week would be vice versa.

What else do you remember about life on the farm?

In the 1930s, our area went through a very dry period. Nothing grew but thistle. Our topsoil blew away, filling many ditches. We did have a garden because we had a good well, and we watered it every day. We had a potato patch in the field, and they didn't even come up. Ontario sent us over a boxcar of apples and dry beans. Nova Scotia sent us salted fish, but no one knew how to use it, so much of it was wasted. Quite a few people just left their places and moved north.

We always had meat while I was growing up because we had our own livestock, but we ate a lot of beans and macaroni. It was no wonder the boys were so ready to enlist when the war broke out – it was a chance to travel and see the world. Everyone thought that we would win, that maybe it would even be over before basic training. We were so wrong in our predictions.

My first job was at Alida General Store. I pumped gas, measured, and bagged sugar, cut and measured cheese

for customers. We sold onions, apples, eggs, nails, screws, pots, pans, and roasters.
Soon after, I got a call saying I had been accepted to try out for Government Telephones in Regina.

What is the biggest way you think farming has changed in your lifetime?

Well, it's gone from horses to big machines. Fertilizing with cow manure to expensive potash, no more summer fallowing, and costly and weird sprays with too many chemicals, in my opinion.

What did you like best about farming when you were younger?

I liked springtime, seeing the seeds start to grow, and I liked harvest. We had a threshing machine and did our farm and neighbours. It was busy, and a full crew stayed in our bunkhouse. We had big meals for breakfast, took lunch to the field in the afternoon, and then had a full supper.

What do you think we as farmers are doing well now?

This is hard because I'm not connected to farming now. It's certainly not the life it used to be. The cost of machinery and how big it is becoming - it seems so money-driven.

What kind of things do you wish we were doing more of?

Reaching out to other people, especially those of other denominations.

Charlie and Benny Keddy, Nova Scotia

Year(s) born: 2012 and 2014

"Kids from Today"

Charlie and Benny Keddy with their parents. Supplied.

What kind of farm do you live on?

Charlie: We grow sweet potatoes, strawberries (plants), and raspberries (plants). We have lots of cows. 60 cows! We use them for meat and make hamburgers that taste really good.

Benny: A big farm! We are a sweet potato farm and strawberries (plants). We have cows too!

What is the best part of living on a farm?

Charlie: I like to drive tractors, and plow and harrow. I like when Dad lets me drive the tractor when we harrow. I like seeing Nana and Poppy all the time. Jumping on hay bales is my favourite. I like washing sweet potatoes and putting the stickers on the boxes.

Benny: Plowing and digging in the dirt. I like driving tractors the best. Oh ya! And Nana always has treats in the office for us. I love treats!

Tell me the best thing about your Mom.

Charlie: I like baling with her, harrowing and eating ice cream with her. Mom is better at baling than Dad is. She always does fun things with us.

Benny: Mom is spelled M-O-M. (He asked me 'Does the lady writing the book know how to spell mom?') She drives tractors. I like driving in the tractor with my Mom.

What is the coolest thing about your Dad?

Charlie: He sneaks us candy and popsicles in the tractor. He knows how to fix the flat tires on our bikes too. He helped me grow my pumpkins to sell. He's a farmer!

Benny: He knows how to fix stuff and makes BIG snow hills with the tractor bucket. I like working with him. Sometimes when Mom's working, he takes us out for breakfast – actually, every time Mom's working. He can push us really high on the swings too!

Have any pets?

Charlie: A cat named Dusty. Two dogs named Tucker and Annie, a horse named Cookie and a donkey that we call Donkey, but his real name is Lucky. I like to look at the chickadees we feed, too, so they are kind of like our pets.

Benny: Cats and dogs and horses and a donkey. When I'm an adult I'm going to have 100 kittens, and they will be so cute. Probably 100 puppies too.

Charlie: No one wants 100 donkeys, though, because when it's time for them to eat, they would be way too loud!

What's the coolest machine on your farm?

Charlie: Definitely the excavator! It can scoop everything up and we can make ditches with it. I even know how to drive it myself. Dad taught me how.

Benny: The sweet potato digger, and the seeder, and the plow and all the tractors and the baler and the excavator. I just like everything.

What do you want to be when you grow up?

Charlie: A farmer and a youtuber. My job on the farm is that I will be the boss. I will tell people what to do and drive all the tractors. I'll grow everything we do now but also pumpkins and Christmas trees. I like to harvest things and make lots of money.

Benny: A farmer. But I'm going to be the boss, not Charlie. He's too bossy.

Are you guys going to farm together when you're adults?

Both: YES!

I might have to buy my own farm too -- but that probably costs a lot of money. Will I have that much money when I'm an adult? Maybe Ben can give me some.

Benny: I will give you some! Then we can have two farms, and we can each be the boss!

"Life with Charlie and Benny" (story from Mom and Dad):

One of our favourite memories of them (ages three and five at the time) is after an enjoyable spring day spent on the farm, playing in the greenhouses, jumping in puddles, and running around, our last job for the day was to feed and bed-down the cows. Both kids love this job and are always eager to help out.

Without fail, though, one or more often than not, both end up falling in the cow barn and getting covered in manure. That day was no different, and after finishing the jobs for the day, we headed to the grocery store nearby to pick up a few things for supper. The employees know the kids well, so seeing them come in wet and dirty at the end of the day was no surprise to them.

One woman, who always made a point to come over and give the kids a hug when she saw them, asked how they had gotten so muddy that day. Charlie gave her a strange look and, matter of factly (and very loudly) said, 'That's not mud! That cow s*it!!'.

"A few of my favourite quotes from them:"
From Mom (Katie Keddy)

Charlie: "Mom, does Santa bring crowbars or machetes?"

On Thanksgiving:

Mom: "What are you most thankful for?"

Charlie: Definitely supper. And ice cream.

Benny: Supper and stuffies. Those are my favourite. Supper was my favourite.

A few moments of quiet

Benny: "I would have been more thankful if I didn't have to share any of my pie with anyone, though."

Charlie leaving his farm stand in the hands of his Dad for a weekend:

'Is Dad going to make sure it stays full? Check the pumpkins? Does he know to take the money in? Refill the straw? He can call if he needs me.'
Ben, running across the lawn to their farm stand screaming at the top of his lungs: 'Another customer!

Yay! It's a Grandma and Grandpa! Yay! They are really old!!!'

Life with boys:

Benny: Mom, when I'm an adult with a cell phone, I'm going to text you and it will say 'Marry me.'

Charlie: Mom, I'll do the same thing ... but it will be a prank so don't get too excited.

Both boys were having a serious discussion about wrenches.

Benny: Allan wrenches are my favourite.

Charlie: *thinks hard and nods in agreement.*

Draw a picture of your family.

Image: Charlie, Age 7

Image: Benny, Age 5

Shane Jones, Alberta

Year born: 1978

"Kid from the 80s"

Photo supplied.

Where did you grow up? How many siblings do you have?

I was born to Shirley and Elwyn Jones in Lloydminster, Saskatchewan and raised on a farm southeast of Paradise Valley, Alberta. I have one sister, Coral, who is four years older.

What kind of farm did you grow up on?

I grew up on a mixed farm of beef cattle and grain. Mom and Dad were kept busy every winter calving out about 100 to 110 cows. While there were a few summer seasons of flax and peas, Dad generally didn't stray too far outside of the lines of barley, wheat, and canola crops.

What key memories and qualities come to mind when you think of your Mom?

My Mom wore many different hats growing up; her roles varied depending on the time of year. She was an incredible role model for us kids as she tried to lead by example. Her love of animals was always apparent. Whether it was the dog, cats, horses or cattle, Mom treated them all like pets (yes, even including the cattle). She was a great partner for my Dad in the cow operation, and to this day knows the lineage of each cow in the pen. As a kid, I could never get my head around how she remembered all this.

One statement that comes to mind regarding my Mom is "always present." As most mothers are, she was always involved in many aspects of my life growing up. From raising and taking care of our daily essentials (for example, cooking and cleaning) to driving my friends and me to copious sporting events all over eastern Alberta and western Saskatchewan, my Mom was always there.

I fondly recall Mom dipping into the big yellow bag of Robin Hood flour while she invested hours making homemade dinner rolls and her infamous cinnamon buns. What kid wouldn't enjoy the spoils of her labour on those days? I also recall when she would make hot meals, and we would load them up for transport to take to my Dad and Uncle Drayson, who were working out in the field. Eating those meals on a sunny warm day while sitting on the end gate of our ½ ton truck, for some reason, always made the food taste better than it already was.

I got my love of sports likely through my Mom. My first television memory is watching the Edmonton Eskimos, a team that she loves to this day. Her passion for playing and watching sports naturally carried over into her, involving me in various practices, clinics, games, and tournaments. I honestly doubt that there was a hockey, fastball, volleyball, basketball, or badminton game that she was not there to witness and be my #1 supporter. For her, the socialization with other farm parents at these sports outings was a major source of enjoyment.

Despite the demands of being a farm wife and a Licensed Practical Nurse (LPN) working in Lloydminster, I remember my Mom investing time with me at the end of a long day when I wanted to grab the ball gloves and play catch in our yard. My Mom was incredibly hard-working, and when it came to her kids, she was (and still is) incredibly selfless with her time.

Tell me about your Dad.

There is no other man on the planet I respect and admire more than my Dad. He is the hardest-working person I know. When Mom and Dad started farming after moving down from Edmonton, he started out with little to no resources. What he initially lacked in land and equipment, he made up for with enthusiasm, passion, hard work, and a desire to provide for his family.

Most young boys look up to their fathers as someone that can do anything, and with my Dad, it wasn't hard to see why. It always seemed to me that there was nothing around the farm that he couldn't do. As a heavy-duty mechanic by trade, he always astounded me with his ability to diagnose and repair basically anything. Most farmers seem to be master problem solvers. My Dad is no different. Looking back on situations that would have left me scratching my head, Dad always seemed to know just what to do.

I always felt growing up that my Dad had the strength of a superhero. Again, most young boys possess the "my dad can beat up your dad" mentality, but I legitimately thought this was true. Looking back, the irony in this line of thinking is that he is the most gentle and kindest person I know. Manners, etiquette and how to behave in general were learnt from watching my Dad. He always puts others first and is generous to a fault.

My Dad is a rancher at heart. Although he loves the life he has built here and now, if he could rewrite his existence, he would likely wish to be born in the late 1800s in the BC interior, during the golden age of British Columbia ranching, or perhaps in the early 1900s, when he could ranch in the foothills of the

Canadian Rockies south of Calgary. Out on the range, in the sun, on a horse watching over a herd of cattle -- this would be his version of heaven on earth.

What was a typical day like for you after you got home from school? What do you remember doing most on the weekends?

A typical post-school day or weekend depended on the time of year. During my younger years, in warmer months, my time was divided between exploring outside with our dog at my side, biking around the farm, riding in the tractor with my Dad, or trying to convince my Mom or sister to engage in some sporting activity with me. I also spent hours in the cool of the basement, shooting pucks and balls into the hockey net that was purchased for me. The dents and markings on the wall indicated that I apparently didn't have very good aim. Younger years or older years, my schedule in the fall and winter was usually held hostage by my busy sports schedule. School sports and the hockey season had to be massaged into a timeline that could accommodate 4-H chores, homework, and general farm help. Typically, after getting home, I would grab the 2-way radio and ask what I could do to help. Dad would normally inquire if I had homework, and if so, I was to get it done first before making my way outside. Both my parents were very considerate and conscientious of me not overextending myself and finding a balance between being a kid and "working" every day.

When the calving season was not in full swing, and there were no hockey tournaments to get to, most Sunday mornings headed into Lloydminster for church. If we were lucky, a meal out with family friends followed, after which we typically enjoyed relaxing for the rest of the afternoon back at the farm.

What would you say was a key activity you did to entertain yourself as a child? As a teen?

Identifying a key activity as a child is difficult as I recall my time being spread out over so many diverse farm activities. Exploring, productively contributing where I could, relaxing with the farm pets, riding my bike, and being given a chance to be a kid all encapsulate early life.

My parents purchased a 300 Honda quad in 1988 (age 10) and with that, I felt my life changed. I wish I would have logged how many hours I spent driving that machine up and down the road, through the pastures, to and from multiple fields and everywhere in between. It allowed me an even greater sense of freedom and independence than I already had. Our three-legged dog at the time, Lacey, would run everywhere with me as we made many miles. Our next dog, Digger, was apparently way smarter, as he would actually ride on the back of the quad no matter where we went. In either case, I always felt like I had a friend with me.

What did you like best about farming when you were younger?

There are so many aspects of farm life that I appreciate now, which I sometimes wonder if I took for granted as a kid since it was the only life I knew.

There was and still is something about the harvest season that brings an excitement that is hard to define. My excitement on a September weekend to make the 10-hour round trip to the farm from Calgary, just to sit on a combine, is something that many of my city friends don't understand. They think I am crazy. The allure of driving a combine in a dusty field (barley crops aside, ha-ha) late into a warm autumn night is something that will always feel nostalgic for me. I realize now that I never felt the weight or pressure of needing to "get the crop off" before the frost or rains came; instead, as a kid, I just got to enjoy being outside under the stars, hearing the hum of the combine in the distance and feeling like I was the luckiest kid in the world. Of course, it may have been my myopic take on things, but to me, these times represented farm life at its best. It just seemed simple and wholesome. Everyone in the family was chipping in and working together for a cause greater than themselves.

As a kid, I loved the freedom that was given to me. There were no real boundaries to constrain a curious farm kid. I felt like I had the best childhood in the world because the best of all worlds surrounded us.

Although I was never good with the mechanics of the machinery that I drove or operated, I enjoyed the time cultivating, harrowing, swathing, harvesting, and driving truck during silage season. I think it made me feel older and more responsible than I know I probably was. But for some reason, my parents had faith that I could do it even when I wasn't sure I could. My Dad still shakes his head at the memory, wondering how he could have allowed it, but I vividly remember operating the forage harvest behind Dad's prized 6030 John Deere tractor. I was just cutting up straw to be collected and eventually mixed with silage for winter feed, but the problem was that I was six years old. To push the clutch in, I would have to brace my back at the edge of the seat and use both legs. The problem was that when I needed to stop, I was unable to put the finicky gear shift into neutral when I was so focused on holding the clutch. Dad's solution was to instruct me to simply pull the kill switch to shut the tractor off when the wagon was full. Once the wagon was dumped into the truck, and I needed to get going, Dad would have to put the tractor in gear for me, engage the PTO and then jump out of the moving tractor. Looking back, we both agree it was sheer lunacy, but it did put a tiny spark of confidence in me that I could do things like that (but not for years later when it was a little more age-appropriate, you know, like age 11 or 12).

Did you feel pressure to continue farming when you grew up?

There was absolutely no pressure to continue with the family farm. I think that both of my parents saw that although I enjoyed farm life, I had other interests and abilities to pursue. I am sure they would have been thrilled had I stated that I intended to follow in their footsteps, but there was absolutely no pressure. Although my parents hid any stress or anxiety they were feeling from my sister and me growing up, it was apparent that farming was an occupation that provided zero guarantees of having dollars in the bank at the end of the year. I remember my parents saying that there is something to having a steady income that isn't based on mother nature. As a result, they were 100 per cent behind my decision to become a Physical Education (PE) Teacher.

How do you feel being raised on a farm helped shape you and your future?

In every way possible!

1. Sense of Community -- As a kid, I loved reading and learning about "Barn Raising Bees" that occurred decades before I was born. The fact that dozens of

people would come together to help a family in need, not expecting anything in return, is an ideal that is both charming and captivating. I loved experiencing the community of Paradise Valley coming together for sporting events, school proms and graduations, funerals (sadly), wedding celebrations, parades and, of course (the highlight of the year, in my opinion) the Paradise Valley Three Cities Fair. Driving on any gravel road and understanding that the person in the ½ tonne truck going the other direction is likely a "neighbour" was somehow comforting. The sense of togetherness that farm life provides despite the isolation (from city standards) has shaped my outlook on people to this day. Everyone in my rural upbringing was always so kind and friendly to everyone else. This selfless, altruistic way of living is what I try to demonstrate not only to my own children, but to the thousands of students I have been able to teach.

2. Work ethic -- There are times as a teacher when I put in 12 to 14-hour days, but I try to remind myself that for farmers, this is a regular occurrence. Seeing how hard both of my parents have worked, it is hard for me to not give the same in my occupation.

3. Appreciation for nature – I often tell my city friends that I could never live in the mountains as I would feel claustrophobic being "closed in." It may seem nonsensical to make such a claim, but nothing makes me more relaxed than the stereotypical "watching the sun go down over a wheat field" scenario. After living in the city of Calgary for 20 years, I try to instill in my own daughters the value of still coming to the farm and hearing the "sound of silence." It may resonate as corny, I know, but the peace and tranquility that rural life brings is something that I currently still cherish.

4. Sports -- Growing up in a rural setting allowed me to be involved in many different things. Going to a small school allowed me to be part of every single sports team that I wished to be part. The confidence this gave me ultimately led me to become the Physical Education (PE) teacher that I am today. I sometimes think that had I grown up in a different environment I would not have embarked on the career that I did. Of course, I am incredibly grateful.

If there was one key thing you wish non-farmers would know about farmers or farming - what do you wish it was?

I am not 100 per cent sure about what I wish non-farmers knew about farming. However, based on my interactions with non-farmers, I get a sense of what many don't know. While I like to think there is often a healthy respect for farmers, I really don't think that a lot of "city-folk" can truly appreciate how difficult farming can be. Throwing some seed in the ground and sitting back to watch it grow while you pitch some hay at the cows is clearly an oversimplified view that some sadly possess. The sheer complexity of many farm operations and the time required for twelve months of the year, is something that even the "somewhat knowledgeable" city dwellers cannot fully grasp. It is a lifestyle that is all-encompassing, but one that most would never want to give up.

I also think it is funny when my Junior High-aged students learn that I grew up on a farm, miles away from my friends and other amenities -- they talk as if they feel sorry for me. They can't imagine how uneventful, boring, and stifling it must have been. If only they knew -- there was nothing better.

What we'd like you to know

We all know that there is a disconnect between rural and urban, farmers and city-dwellers, producers and consumers. Coming from a primarily city-living background to being immersed in farm life now for more than a decade - I would summarize the disconnection as the following:

- Farmers are not poisoning you through your food
- They are making a conscious decision to live this life, it's not the "only thing "they know how to do
- They love and are attached to the land they farm. They are long-time family-run businesses, not "factory farms "
- That farming requires knowledge of science and math, along with skills in planning, organizing, marketing, technology, and research
- the sheer volume of market terms being used to make you believe that what you're purchasing is better than what we are providing already.

But this section isn't about what *I* think.

One day in the fall of 2020, I posted the following question to social media:

"If there was one thing you wish non-farmers knew about us - what would it be?"

Over 4,000 people engaged with that post. This is what just some of them said:

- *We are people, just like you. We care about what our kids eat, the world they live in, and the future they will be left with. We love our livestock and treat them with respect; after all, they are the reason we can eat and pay the bills.*

- *We need consumers to stand with us. We live a lifestyle and a job with no start or end time to feed the masses. Our pay is minimal, and sometimes it's not enough to cover the months' bills, but we keep going because that is the job we chose to do, and this is what we love.*

- *Most farmers have a calling. They aren't in it for the money or the glory. Farming is dirty, backbreaking, and never-ending work. My Dad would wake at 4 a.m. to milk the cows and often be in the field until midnight.*

- *Farmers enjoy seeing their labour produce results: the calf growing into a cow, the wheat being sowed, the hay being baled. While most people never think about it - without farmers, we wouldn't eat.*

- *I want people to know that farmers don't get a break when they're sick animals still need food and care. If you're up late visiting, you're still up at the crack of dawn. When you lose an animal, you lose a paycheck, and you will have to sell that extra twin calf to make up for it. There are usually no extras to be had, and most farmers don't retire at 65 - they farm until the end because they don't know what to do with retirement. They've worked all their lives.*

- *Our lives see the trees like city folks see skyscrapers. Eagles are the noisy air traffic overhead. The world can't afford to lose us. We need your support. Our survival is your prosperity.*

- *I wish non-farmers knew the amount and extent of daily work required and that we can't just leave the farm whenever we feel like it. I also want non-farmers to know that sitting around visiting takes away from the time we need to allocate to farm projects.*

- *We invest our whole lives in this. We spend our entire lives passionately learning as much as possible, a lot of it by experience, and it's degrading to us when they come in and tell us what we should be doing. Please work with us, not against us.*

- *Farming is what we do. Everything needs to work together from home to the field to run properly. As a farmwife, I'm just as important as the farmer. When he is gone long hours, I manage the household duties alone; I take meals to the field, help move equipment, do parts runs that sometimes take six hours for a round trip and work off the farm in a nursing home. My life isn't leisurely and slack. Things need to be planned and organized, but I also have to fly by the seat of my pants simultaneously! This is our life, and it's a great life!!*

- *When other women hear that I'm a stay-at-home farmwife and mom, they think I have an easy and lazy life. That is not at all true. From spring to fall, I am a single mother of three kids. I homeschool, clean and cook. I take lunches to the field and help move equipment from field to field. I drive grain cart all fall. I think I'm busier than my husband.*

- *Just because we know the ending to an animal's life and that we do it for profit doesn't mean we don't care and do everything we can to ensure a stress-free quality of life while they are alive*

- *I wish non-farmers knew that farming is not a job, it is a lifestyle, and more often than not, the farm comes first. It doesn't mean we don't like vacations, we don't want to visit, we don't want time off, but this job is not one where you can just take off and leave it for a few days. It is 24/7 and demanding. It controls all aspects of your life.*

- *That the time, effort, energy, work, love, and money put into everything is much greater than they can imagine.*

- *That industry has stood between farmers and consumers. We need to have coffee and ask what each of us can do to make life better for one another. Industry, as the go between, is not working.*

- *That farmers really do care about their animals*

- *We do this because we love this life, not because we can't do anything else.*

- *Whether it be livestock, grain, or fruits and vegetables - it's the way of life and giving back we love. There is nothing more rewarding than having that calf, lamb, or the fields with great yields. It's about knowing you are helping someone eat after your harvest. It's a lifestyle that comes with great rewards and great downfalls. You learn to take the good with the bad, and you never take anything for granted.*

- *What I wish people knew is that farmers do not set the price they are paid for what they produce. When there are big jumps in proces at the grocery stores, it's not the farmers fault.*

- *I wish more people were patient when I'm driving that big piece of equipment down the highway slowly. I'm not trying to slow you down, I'm trying to be safe with my own life, and yours.*

- *Farmers buy at retail, sell at wholesale, and hope to break even. We are not rich in money, but rich in lifestyle and pride. It's a unique feeling to plant a post in the ground in the same place your grandfather did 70 years ago.*

- *Oh, and NO we don't all wear straw hats, bibs and rubber boots*

- *We work morning and night, 7 days per week, whether we are sick or not*

- *Whether it be livestock, grain, or fruits and vegetables - it's the way of life and giving back we love. There is nothing more rewarding than having that calf, lamb, or the fields with great yields. It's about knowing you are helping someone eat after your harvest. It's a lifestyle that comes with great rewards and great downfalls. You learn to take the good with the bad, and you never take anything for granted.*

- *Whether it be livestock, grain, or fruits and vegetables - it's the way of life and giving back we love. Nothing is more rewarding than having that calf, lamb, or the fields with great yields. It's about knowing you are helping someone eat after your harvest. It's a lifestyle that comes with great rewards and great downfalls. You learn to take the good with the bad, and you never take anything for granted.*

- *I wish non-farmers understood that we could not profit from sick or abused animals, so the farmers need and depend on the health and well-being of their animals to provide for their families.*

- *We love our animals and give them very good care. They have good lives. They also have a purpose, and that purpose is food. A farmer can provide humane care and have affection for livestock and still harvest them.*

- *Because many farm kids start helping on the farm at a young age, they learn more about compassion, responsibility, and creativity. For example, when you don't have the strength to lift 50-pound bags, they have to think of other ways to get things done. They learn math (how much seed do we need to plant that 50-acre field)? They learn science (what's the best feed mix for each season)? That's something most people never even think about.*

- *Our animals are fed, watered and bedded down before we eat, shower and rest. Every single day is governed by the weather. We plant expensive seed, and wait. The weather makes us successful, or it can literally break us.*

- *During birthing season we do late-night barn checks, sometimes in frigid temperatures. We are the veterinarian, the midwife, and the Emergency Medical Technician (EMT).*

- *The Ag Community is like no other! We are a family of our own. We do whatever it takes to ensure our farm friends have what they need to do the job. If my neighbour's machine breaks down, I'll take mine and finish the job. That's just one small example of how special our ag community is!*

- *I wish people really knew what a GMO is and why they're used.*

- *I wish non-farmers knew this is not just a "job". This is a passion and it's what made us who we are. Our family farms have been passed down through generations. Or, we have started our little slice of heaven through years of hard work to build what we have.*

- *We are strong, we are resilient, and we are the eternal optimist. We will keep working, and we will put our all into everything again next year. And the year after that.*

- *If I could, I would tell them, if you don't know what or how something is done or why we do things the way we do, ask. But if you ask, be prepared to listen with an open mind.*

- *That just because my dogs live outside doesn't mean I don't love them*

- *We don't get any days off (sick or vacation), but we wouldn't trade our lifestyle for anything*

- *We are humans like everyone else, and no we are not trying to kill you*

- *Coming from a non-farming family that married a farmer, there is a completely different mindset when it comes to the world (and basically everything). Farmers are some of the smartest, most resourceful, and hardest-working people on the planet!*

- *Farmers care so much. About the land, soil, environment, family, having a successful business, keeping up with technology and science, and that the food we produce is the best it can be for the consumer. We wish people would talk to a farmer before judging what they see in a documentary.*

- *How much love and devotion we put into this lifestyle AND how most LARGE farms that have multiple employees are STILL family farms. Also we take pride in our product and always want the gap between urban and rural to become smaller! Education is key!*

- *How much we love our land and our animals. And if ever there were advocates for our environment and animals - it would be us farmers! The care and pride that go into both is something that is just not understood by a lot of people with no farming background. It's so sad that there is such a disconnect in society from the truth about where and how the worlds food is produced.*

- *We are the best stewards of the land there is anywhere. Without our land being healthy we wouldn't be able to raise animals or grow crops. Without healthy land we wouldn't be able to make a living. We are always trying to improve the way we manage the land.*

- *That we don't get the handouts that people think we do.*

- *That we are NOT poisoning them or receiving money from big companies as a cover for something.*

- *Don't blame us for all the pollution. We aren't trying to kill you, cause your children to mature faster, cause your food sensitivities, or cause you to be resistant to antibiotics.*

- *There has never been a time in history when we have enjoyed such a secure food supply and food safety. We take great pride in supplying safe, nutritious, and accessible food for all Canadians and many other nations worldwide.*

- *That 'organic' and 'non-GMO' are marketing terms.*

- *How cattle contribute to the ecosystem, not destroy it*
- *Our crops aren't drenched in chemicals; we put a great deal of thought into which one we use*
- *We are very tired and grouchy in September*

In the End

If we're being honest, none of us know down the road if our kids will remain in the same way of life that we're raising them in. After all, it's a big world out there.

Wherever they end up in their life – may our kids always know who they are, where they came from and where home was.

A Final Note

It is too easy to forget that we were not the first people on this land.

The land where we farm in northeastern Alberta (Treaty 6 Territory) was taken from the Plains Cree, Woodland Cree, Saulteaux, Blackfoot, Métis, Dene, and Nakota Sioux people, who were the original caretakers of this land.

Indigenous People throughout history have been terrorized and displaced, but they not only still survive, but they are sharing their stories.

I believe it's our honour to listen to them and live among them.

- Billi.

Acknowledgments

Thank you first to my friends and readers for their patience as I had to delay my intended release date for this book from March 2022 to December 2022. I hope it is worth your wait.

To my husband, Dean. Even though you wouldn't let me put you in this book, you are truly the ultimate farm kid. I'm so happy you're my husband. To Madeline, and Kate for their non-stop inspiration. You're my favourite farm kids of all.

Thanks to Jennifer Blair for her assistance in editing this book. To Elaine Froese, friend, and mentor. To Get It Done Productions (Alex & Lindsey) for your endless motivation. And, to my friend Lisa Guenther for making me believe I have good stories to tell.

Thanks to my sister and extended family for your support and care.

Love, endless respect, and thanks to my group of seven for being my biggest fans.

Lastly, to my community: you fill my heart, make me smile, make me laugh, and give me so much joy to live among you.

About the Author:

Billi is an author, photographer, speaker, and writer from east-central Alberta, Canada (near Lloydminster). Previously a city-living, nine-to-five Government worker, Billi moved to the country to marry Dean in 2010 and traded concrete and traffic for life on a 100-year-old prairie farm. Quickly falling in love with her new surroundings, thick with deep roots and a long history, she harnessed her entrepreneurial spirit by creating a successful freelance writer and photographer business.

In 2016, she authored the first of a two-book series about the remarkable contributions of farmwives and has been recognized for her work on CBC, Global TV, City TV, and countless newspapers and magazines in Canada and the US.

In 2020 (during the pandemic), she published her third book (her first "children's book") with her daughters about their family dog. "Farm Kids: Stories from Our Lives" is Miller's fourth book. Miller has truly found her passion for "telling stories from the heart and telling stories that matter." Billi resides with her husband and two young girls on a 111-year-old farm where she works from her home office, her favourite coffee shop, or the road.

Other Books from the Author:

Farmwives in Profile: 17 Women, 17 Candid Questions About their Lives, Photos & Recipes

Billi J. Miller

When Billi married her husband, a 4th generation Canadian farmer, she quickly discovered there were very little photographs of their rich, 100-year farming heritage. As a writer + photographer, she felt called to do something about it. Since relocating in 2010 to the country from the big city: she was taken aback by the amazing contributions of the farmwives, not only in their homes and in their families - but, in their communities. This book celebrates them, their life's work, and their passionate dedication to the larger patchwork of

Canada's Heritage. Farmwives in Profile is a labour of love "heart project" for Billi J Miller that blends heartfelt Q + As about each woman's life as a farmwife, beautiful photos, and of course, recipes! As a touching tribute to them, some of the families have included a piece as to the impact their Mom has had on their lives. This book serves as both a lasting legacy for those that live here, as well as an intimate and culinary look into life on the Canadian Prairies for those that do not.

Farmwives 2: An Inspiring Look into the Lives of the New Canadian Farmwives

Billi J. Miller

In January 2016, Billi J Miller launched her first published book (a four-and-a-half-year labour of love) celebrating "traditional" farmwives (between the ages of fifty-five and ninety) for their remarkable contributions to their families, farms, and to the wider scope of Canadian heritage. Farmwives in Profile: 17 Women, 17 Candid Questions about their Lives, Photos & Recipes has been hailed a "gem" for its candid stories, delicious straight-from-the-farm-kitchen recipes, and Miller's timeless photographs of the women.

Now it's the "next generations" turn. Farmwives 2: An Inspiring Look at the Lives of the New

Canadian Farmwives is the highly anticipated follow-up that homes in on women in their twenties to fifties. This time, Miller interviews women from across the country- from British Columbia all the way to Newfoundland- broadening not only the look at Canada's family farms but, women's perspectives on this evolving role.

"Farmwives 2" is loaded with all-new recipes, many more inspiring interviews, and features a special "Food for Thought" section filled with input by professionals you won't want to miss. Miller says she walked into this life eight years ago with no guidebook other than very traditional farmwives all around her, and a feeling in her gut that told her she had to make her life her own. This book is packed with interviews and stories from inspiring women from across Canada who are doing that very thing.

Bubbles Took a Trip: A Mostly True Tale About an Adventurous Dog from the Canadian Prairies

Billi J. Miller

Fall in love with "Bubbles" the real-life Bernese Mountain Dog in this book titled: "Bubbles Took a Trip: A Mostly True Tale About an Adventurous Dog from the Canadian Prairies". This true story is told by Author Billi J. Miller with her daughters Madeline and Kate about their beloved family pet. The story tells the tale about Bubbles being "accidentally dog-napped" one day by a nice lady who was worried about her being on the highway near her farm. Not knowing who her owners were, the woman drove Bubbles to her home (four hours away). This is the story about Bubbles' adventure and how her family got her back.

billi j. miller

author
photographer
speaker

Telling stories from **the heart**... telling stories **that matter.**

www.billijmiller.com

www.ingramcontent.com/pod-product-compliance
Lightning Source LLC
Chambersburg PA
CBHW040227170726
48295CB00014B/834

* 9 7 8 1 7 7 7 4 1 8 6 4 9 *